## NEW LIFE JOKE SHOP
Travels & Observations

# NEW LIFE JOKE SHOP
Travels & Observations

# YOSEF WOSK

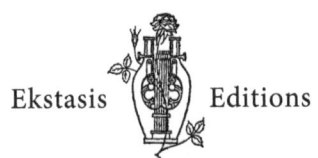

Ekstasis Editions

Copyright © Yosef Wosk 2025
Cover Art: Fred Herzog, New Life Joke Shop, Vancouver, 1957. *Courtesy of The Estate of Fred Herzog and Equinox Gallery, Vancouver.* © *The Estate of Fred Herzog, 2024.*
Auhor photo: Shelley Karrel
Design: Derek von Essen
Published in 2025 by:
Ekstasis Editions Canada Ltd. Box 8474, Main Postal Outlet Victoria, B.C. V8W 3S1

All rights reserved. No part of this book may be reproduced in any form without the written permission of the publisher, with the exception of brief passages in reviews. Any request for photocopying or other reproduction of any part of this book should be directed in writing to the publisher or to ACCESS: The Canadian Copyright Licensing Agency, One Yonge Street, Suite 800, Toronto, Ontario, Canada, M5E 1E5.


Library and Archives Canada Cataloguing in Publication

Title: New life joke shop / Yosef Wosk.
Names: Wosk, Yosef, author
Description: First edition.
Identifiers: Canadiana (print) 2024047614X | Canadiana (hardcover) 20240476158 | ISBN 9781771715805 (softcover) | ISBN 9781771715812 (HARDCOVER)
Subjects: LCGFT: Essays.
Classification: LCC PS8645.O85 N49 2025 | DDC C814/.6—dc23

To Avi, Rahel & Shevi

*"We are a river without banks in a world without borders,*
*soul-soaked in jasmine and rose,*
*flying on the wings of forever."*
— Y.W.

CONTENTS

| | |
|---|---|
| 9 | *Introduction* |
| 15 | My Life as a Spy |
| 45 | New Life Joke Shop |
| 87 | The Future of Knowledge |
| 103 | Oroboros |
| 115 | Reflections Upon Turning Seventy |
| 137 | Old Men Ought to Be Explorers |
| 161 | Five Blessings and a Dare |
| 167 | Nasreddin |
| 169 | Three Poems (Haida Gwaii) |
| 171 | *Endnotes* |
| 195 | *Biography* |

Fred Herzog, New Life Joke Shop, Vancouver, 1957. *Courtesy of The Estate of Fred Herzog and Equinox Gallery, Vancouver.* © *The Estate of Fred Herzog, 2024.*

# INTRODUCTION

*Wosk & Wong*

The title *New Life Joke Shop* is derived from a black & white photograph taken in Vancouver's Chinatown, by the venerable Fred Herzog, in 1957. It is a remarkable photograph of a mundane subject—a man gazing through the window of a novelty shop and variety store.

Much more is revealed, however, by looking carefully at the picture. Two things immediately caught my attention and prompted me to purchase this captivating image: 1) the general feeling of nostalgia, and 2) the words printed on the awning and storefront window.

*New Life*, along with the Chinese calligraphy, indicates that the owner was an immigrant who dedicated himself to a fresh beginning in Canada.

*Joke Shop* reveals the proprietor's good sense of humour and lends an atmosphere of joy to the establishment.

John Atkin, Vancouver heritage consultant and civic historian extraordinaire, was able to identify the location of the store along with the name of its owner and an accompanying anecdote. We discovered that it was only two blocks from my family's furniture and appliances main store, Wosk's Ltd., at 62 West Hastings, a location that I visited often as a child and where I worked part-time as a teen.

John Atkin writes:

> The New Life Joke Shop/Confectionery was at 420 Columbia Street just in from Hastings Street on the east side of Columbia. The proprietor of the shop when the photo was taken was a Harry Wong. He foiled a robbery attempt in 1958 when a man walked into the store with his hands in his coat pocket saying he had a gun. Wong ignored the robber, picked up the phone on the wall behind him, dialed a number and just spoke into the receiver, saying there was a robbery and a car should be sent immediately. The would-be robber fled as the fake call was made.
>
> The building is still standing and today it is used by a Clan Association, for meetings and housing for its members. The storefront survives, albeit without the 1950s signage.

In the image, the storefront is impeccably maintained. There is an assortment of signs and a neat-although-crowded display of goods; the sidewalk [surprisingly decorated with tiles or thick translucent glass apertures designed to allow light into the basement below] is swept; the awning is clean and the window is washed.

The customer gazing through the window is dressed in a clean, all-black suit and hat with polished dark shoes. His face, sheathed in shadow, serves to continue the black vertical line of the anonymous figure.

The knot securing the awning is expertly tied, something that adds stability, even a perception of confidence, to the image, while the inventory appears to be ample and of a great variety. We assume *New Life Joke Shop* offers an overflowing cornucopia of products including some food such as confectioneries [candy, chocolate, gum, dried fruit and perhaps sweet baked goods]; Kik, Coke and Pepsi sodas; in addition to tobacco, newspapers and magazines, jokes, coins and stamps, as well as a wide assortment of novelties.

Look again at the customer—at his feet. One foot is firmly planted in front of the window but the other one is pointed to his right as if to say, "That's enough dawdling. Time to move on." It is an age-old conflict extending from birth until death do us part: whether to stay or move on. You can almost hear him thinking as he hesitates for another minute or two, staring intently at the items, perhaps at some of the "foreign stamps," a reminder of home or a trophy to be added to his collection.

Maybe it's an information bulletin he's reading? Or is he catching a forbidden glance at a pin-up featured on the *Modern Sunbathing and Hygiene* nudist magazines also displayed in the store that sells all to everyone?

If you look closely at the Emporium, you do see some "naturist" magazines in the window. In those days, Vancouver was a fairly strait-laced, racist, provincial town but if you dared to venture towards Chinatown you might be able to enter a local confectionery and pick up a 1950s softcore-erotic novel, such as *When Bad Women Walked Good Dogs*, possibly in a cellophane protective sleeve. When I was about thirteen years old, a cousin showed me his secret stack of *Sunbathing Magazines*, the exact sort that were on display in Harry Wong's window.

The address over the door is in brass numerals, faintly repeated on the glass door, 420, a number that carries many symbolic meanings from sources as diverse as the Bible, Tarot, Numerology and Cannabis Culture.[1] What really lays beyond the step-up threshold leading to the inviting door?

For those with a literary bent, peering into the dizzying shop window transports us to Hermann Hesse's novel *Steppenwolf* wherein the protagonist encounters the "Magic Theatre. Not for everyone. For Madmen Only."[2]

We are that man; Joke Shop is the world. And so, we market ourselves. We are all products looking for homes but may never know who picks us up from merchandise shelves and then thinks they own us, as they proceed to domesticate and train us, and demand that we worship them in our mutual madness here in the deep end of life. We all harbour universal chaos beneath a veneer of carefully curated respectability, and we, like the three-ring Circus Master or Harry Wong, control those elemental forces for fear of the consequences. At least most of the time; at least most of us.

This could have been Fred Herzog's intuitive inspiration when he took the photo with black & white film instead of colour (for which his work is now internationally renowned).

Ulrich Herzog (the name "Fred" came later, in Canada) was born in the German town of Bad Friedrichshall in 1930 and grew up in Stuttgart. In 1941, during World War II, his mother died from typhoid and, five years later, his father, who had been traumatised by the war, also passed away.[3] Herzog immigrated to Canada in 1952 and the following year he arrived in Vancouver where he pioneered "street photography" with minimal recognition until the 1990s. A retrospective exhibition, *Fred Herzog: Vancouver Photographs*, was eventually held at the Vancouver Art Gallery in 2007.

In 2014, Herzog's photograph *Bogner's Grocery* (1960) was released as a limited edition stamp as part of Canada Post's Canadian Photography Series. The image is reminiscent of our lesser-known *New World Joke Shop*, a photo that had been lost in a collection of his black & white archives. Herzog died in 2019, almost 89 years old.

This entire book mimics the shop window. These literary offerings are my confections, jokes, reflections and novelties. In a separate chapter, also called *New World Joke Shop,* you will find thirty-one definitions, observations or mini-essays in the context of a general store. Enter 420, get lost and settle in for an adventure through the looking glass. Step right up and get your Ticket to Ride. You have nothing to lose but your sanity and nothing to gain but your mind.

Yours,
Wosk & Wong
aka *Erasmus Filius Philosophorum*[4]

In 1977, as a neophyte spy in Russia, the KGB-influenced Intourist agency billeted us at the world's largest hotel (from 1967 to 1980), the Hotel Rossiya, in one of its 3,182 bugged rooms. It closed in 2006.

# MY LIFE AS A SPY

The rallying cry of "Let My People Go"—dating back 3500 years, to when Moses negotiated with the pharoah to let the enslaved Jewish nation depart from Egypt—once again echoed around the world in the 1970s when Russia and the West were engaged in the Cold War.

That's why, in 1977, I volunteered to go on a covert mission behind the Iron Curtain to make contact with the refuseniks—Jews stuck inside the former Soviet Union who were being refused permission to emigrate, either to Israel or another free country.

My task was not to liberate these despondent Jews who were oppressed by silence and disinformation, economic hardship, authoritarian detention and cultural annihilation, but rather to bring them news from the outside world and to reassure them that they were not forgotten.

This enterprise was not just frowned upon by the Russians: it was illegal. If discovered, my travel partner from Detroit, Shmuel Gordon, and I would likely be detoured into a Russian prison.

Shmuel, who had been my *hevrusa* (talmudic study colleague), and I embarked on this stealthy mission armed with nothing more than our wits and intentions, although I did have some basic weapons training. My involvement with firearms began four years earlier when, as a seminary student in Jerusalem, I carried a rifle as an auxiliary police guard night-patrolling our neighbourhood in the wake of the 1973 Yom Kippur War when terrorists were threatening the community.

Two years later, upon enrolling at Yeshiva University in New York, I joined two clubs: the Karate Club and the Gun Club. Every few weeks, a group of us—bespectacled, peace-loving, bearded students in our twenties—dutifully tumbled into our sponsor's battered urban chariot for the long drive to an indoor rifle range in the Bronx. This went on for a year. It felt like this was the least we could do to prepare ourselves for the unwelcome but seemingly inevitable conflicts that pursue our people in every generation.

I was soon to discover that, for Jews or political dissidents, life inside the USSR was like dwelling at the Hotel California[5] where "you can check out anytime you like, but you can never leave." Defecting was difficult; legal emigration from the imprisoned state was almost impossible.

I make no claim that my mission was anything like some adrenalin-rush, Tom Cruise movie. Our task was to lay low, not to be flying high. But if I had known at the time how dangerous our diplomatic outreach to the Soviet Union was going to be, I might not have signed up for it. I lived to tell the tale but this is the first time I've shared it. My three children, to whom this book is dedicated, are learning about this story for the first time.

Only a small group of rabbinical students volunteered for this assignment. We were interviewed twice. The first interview was conducted by a senior tutor at the university. His grandparents had emigrated from Russia in the 1920s and helped to re-establish orthodox education in both Israel and the United States, especially in Chicago.

A week later we were informed that we were deemed appropriate for the mission but that we'd still have to meet a representative of the sponsoring organization. If he also liked what he saw—how we looked, spoke, thought and presented ourselves under duress—then we'd be accepted for the overseas operation.

Shmuel and I boarded the A-train subway from Washington Heights where we lived in the yeshiva dorms, then transferred at Rockefeller Centre in mid-town Manhattan for another hour's ride to Brighton Beach, aka "Little Odessa," just down the promenade from Coney Island in Brooklyn. That's where we were told to meet our handler at a nondescript motel at 10 a.m. on a Tuesday winter's morning.

We arrived just in time and waited for him to greet us in the lobby. But he wasn't there. We waited nervously for another ten minutes, reluctant to approach the clerk to ask if our cloak-and-dagger field agent was registered there. We double-checked the address before finally deciding to take a chance—even though it might have blown his cover—and mentioned his name. Without batting an eye or even having to look up the information, the clerk nodded, gave us the room number and pointed the way just down the hall on the first floor.

When we knocked on his door and identified ourselves, our contact let us in and began the conversation by scolding us for being late. "If you can't keep an appointment over here," he rebuked us in what sounded like an Israeli accent, "how can I trust you to carry out the work over there?"

Mortified that the mission might be aborted before it even began, we apologized and explained that we didn't want to mention his name to the motel staff in order to protect his identity. He then proceeded to interview us and, when satisfied of our near-competence, he instructed us in some well-earned spy-craft techniques.

In the ensuing years I realized that Shmuel and I had just participated in a real-life enactment of a famous joke.

A guy [a favourite term used by English-speaking Russians] gets a job as a spy. He's sent on his first mission and told that the secret password he has to give to contacts is, "The night-bird flies at dawn."

He's instructed to go to London, head to Piccadilly Circus and speak to a guy in a purple fedora, busking. So he flies to London, goes to Piccadilly Circus, finds a busker with a purple fedora and says to him, "The night-bird flies at dawn."

The busker replies, "Right mate! Now you need to go to Paris and talk to a guy sitting under the Eiffel Tower, painting a picture of eggplants."

So off to Paris he goes, down to the Eiffel Tower and he sees someone sitting under it painting a picture of eggplants.

"The night-bird flies at dawn."

"Ahh! Oui, oui! Zee night-bird! Next you must go to New York, Greenwich Village, 177A Bleecker Street, and speak to a man named Goldberg."

He proceeds to New York, Greenwich Village, 177A Bleecker Street. He looks at the mailboxes and sees "Goldberg 2B."

He knocks on the door and when someone answers it he says, "The night-bird flies at dawn."

The guy, clearly annoyed, rolls his eyes and says, "No, no, no! You want Goldberg the spy. He's in 5C."

Our Brooklyn mentor in the ways of espionage warned us about a number of obstacles that we were bound to encounter, including:

- Every hotel room that would be assigned to us would be bugged so that agents could monitor our conversations, determine our intentions and gather information that could be used against us or other collaborators.

- Telephones would also be wiretapped so no conversations could be assumed to be private. This was twenty years before email and the Internet became widely used so communication devices and other tracking techniques were limited.

- Do not carry contact logistics in an easily discoverable manner such as having names and numbers of refuseniks printed on a sheet of paper.

- You may be apprehended and questioned as to your true purpose for visiting the USSR. You may be accused of subversive activity and could be arrested, imprisoned or deported.

- Those who you visit may also be detained, interrogated and probably arrested in order to further intimidate them.

As I recall, a number of tactics were employed to offset Soviet surveillance capabilities:

- When we wanted to make plans to visit refuseniks, Shmuel and I used three techniques: Either write on magic slates[6] we brought for the occasion, low-tech temporary messages that could then be easily made to vanish; go for a walk outside where we could converse without being eavesdropped upon; or put on some music in the room to act as a cover as we quickly exchanged our thoughts in a voice too low to be audible to secret police recording devices.

- As for contact logistics: Unless we had photographic memories it would have been impossible to memorize the names, phone numbers and addresses we were given. Instead, we were instructed to use an extra fine ballpoint pen to record the information in small letters and numerals on random pages in the gutter of a book where the pages are bound together. When someone casually flipped through the book searching for notes hidden among the pages, they would not notice the tiny script stealthily concealed therein, effectively hiding in plain sight. I took an abridged paperback edition of *The 1001 Arabian Nights* that I purchased at Barnes & Noble. A classic collation of centuries of Middle Eastern and Asian folktales originally written in Arabic but available in a number of translations, it was filled with violence, intrigue and sex but I chose it as another cover for my identity as well as for the adventure I imagined it contained.

- As for the eventuality of being apprehended and cross-examined as to our true purpose for visiting the USSR, we were directed to insist that we were merely tourists, university students curious about Russian history and culture with no subversive intentions. We were somewhat apprehensive about being detained and I could feel the tension accumulating as each day of our journey into the heart of the "Evil Empire"[7] continued to unfold. It was only years later that humour, once again, offered its balm of perspective and relief. I was reminded of the advice extended in Neil Simon's play *The Odd Couple,* when Felix advises Oscar that if he was ever accused of having an extra-marital affair, to "Deny, deny, deny." And of the famous line attributed to Groucho Marx: "Who are you going to believe? Me or your lying eyes?"[8] Such advice may not have amused the KGB but it sure would have buoyed us as we sent postcards from Siberia.

Our mentor also advised us not to wear overt Jewish symbols such as a kippah head covering or a Star of David necklace, what to bring with us to present to those we were to meet, and how to behave at Russian border crossings.

Three months later, we found ourselves flying from New York to Moscow on Lufthansa through Frankfurt, an ironic arrangement that had us passing through the gates of a former Merchant of Doom on the way to the present Unforgiving Gulag. Fearing antisemitism as well as KGB agents surveilling us, we removed our kippahs in the German hub and didn't wear them again in public until returning to New York almost two weeks later.

The general reader needs to be aware that in living memory the Russian Jewish Community had suffered greatly through pogroms, two World Wars, the Bolshevik Revolution (that turned into a Communist dictatorship), the Holocaust and then during exile to new countries seeking hoped-for peace.

It is also regrettably necessary to mention that out of a global population of approximately 18,000,000 Jews before WW II, approximately 6,000,000 Jewish people were murdered by the German Nazis and their collaborators during the Shoah [the Hebrew word for the Holocaust], including 1,300,000 Soviet Jewish civilians. In addition, hundreds of thousands of other Jews died during the various conflicts, including pogroms and famines.

Eighty years after the War, the worldwide Jewish population, now estimated to be just over fifteen million, has still not fully recovered.

Antisemitism in the Soviet Union sought to suppress Jewish religious traditions, education and culture. As an atheistic and later antisemitic state, the Communist regime—not unlike the Nazis—shamelessly confiscated religious and cultural properties as they arrested, exiled and executed members of the community in an effort to totally liquidate Jewish identity and assimilate the population under the banner of Marxist ideals. One could argue that the state did not discriminate in the application of its draconian policies, for their acts of cultural genocide were repeated against all other religions and ethnic minorities.

During the 20th century, millions of Jews emigrated from various European as well as Islamic countries to other parts of the world including North America, Australia, South America, South Africa and even to other European locations. With the re-establishment of the State of Israel in 1948 a new haven was created. In 1977, two million persecuted Jews trapped inside the Soviet Union could not wait to be liberated.

The general Russian population had also suffered on an industrial scale.

[At the time of our visit I didn't have easy access to these hugely relevant statistics estimating that up to 61,300,000 Russians had been killed, either directly or as a result of intentional policies, through a series of both internal and global conflicts in the 20$^{th}$ century.]

*Estimated Total Russian Casualties*

- *World War I* [1914–1918] — 1,800,000 soldiers and 1,500,000 civilians.

- *Russian Civil War* [Bolshevik Revolution, 1917–1923] — 7,000,000 to 12,000,000 casualties, mostly civilian.

- *Soviet regime of Joseph Stalin* [c. 1928–1953] — Number of deaths attributed to direct action or as a result of policies such as executions, destruction of population through man-made famines, and deaths during forced deportations, imprisonment and forced labor, are estimated at 6,000,000 to 20,000,000 or higher.

- *World War II* [The Great Patriotic War 1941–1945] — Up to an estimated 26,000,000 Soviet citizens, including as many as 11,000,000 soldiers.[9]

But I did know about the Russian empire. Over the years, family lore had taught me much more than statistics....

Previous generations of my family had first-hand experiences with many of the conflicts. My father was born in Odessa, Ukraine, then part of the Russian Empire, in November 1917, in the shadow of the Bolshevik Revolution. In spite of his grandfather, the family patriarch, having being forced to serve 25 years in the czar's army and then being permitted to be a landowner, the family, along with fellow Jews, was subject to pogroms, wars, land confiscation, harsh taxes and redistribution of wealth, crop failures, conscription and antisemitism. Our branch of the family immigrated to Canada in 1928. Most other relatives remained behind: hundreds perished; all suffered.[10]

My mother's side of the family had also escaped from antisemitic persecution in Pinsk, Poland, now Belarus. A dark secret that we were warned to conceal for fear of retribution from the NKVD, Stalin's Secret Police, was that we were related to Leon Trotsky [Lev Davidovich Bronstein], revolutionary politician, founder of the Red Army and one of the heirs apparent to Lenin for leadership of the USSR. Stalin [Iosif Vissarionovich Dzhugashvili], in his purge of challengers, had Trotsky assassinated in Mexico where he sought refuge in the home of Diego Rivera and Frida Khalo.

Before embarking on the mission, I told my parents of our intended plans, assuming they might be proud of me and support the operation. Perhaps, I naively thought, it would even be a kind of catharsis for all they had suffered.

Instead, my parents were vehemently opposed to my returning to the killing fields of Eastern Europe from which they had precariously escaped. They were concerned that harm awaited and that it was a foolish risk to take.

In a final effort to convince me to abandon my cavalier plans, my mother had even declared: "If you go, I won't be your mother anymore!"

I was shocked for a moment but remained determined in my resolve for three reasons: 1) I had already made a commitment; 2) as an idealistic young man I wanted to be involved in just such a dedicated venture to serve my people; and 3) it gave me a sense of independence, a voice of my own.

## Welcome to Moscow

We arrived at Moscow's Sheremetyevo airport at the end of March 1977, a few days before the Passover holiday. A late Spring snow covered the tarmac as we made our way into the terminal. Anatoly Shcharansky [Natan Sharansky], the human-rights activist and most prominent refusenik, had just been arrested and tensions were high.[11]

Our luggage was thoroughly searched at customs. Officials demanded to know why we brought so many books as well as so much kosher food. The books—religious texts and general interest volumes on Jewish subjects—were meant as gifts for refuseniks but we insisted that they were for personal use. We packed the extra kosher food (including matzah, gefilte fish, horseradish and dried fruit) because of special dietary restrictions during Passover and we knew that such provisions would not be available in the country. The KGB border guards isolated us, accused us of trying to smuggle contraband into the country, threatened to confiscate all the items and to deport us on the next available plane. It seemed that, once again, our mission was doomed before it even began.

After arguing for half an hour, our assigned Intourist guide appeared, assisted with the customs procedure and bundled us into the waiting Lada for the trip to the hotel.

We were billeted in the Rossiya Hotel, a massive structure comprising four 12-storey buildings at least a country-block long in every direction constructed around a central courtyard. I later learned that when it was built it was the largest hotel in the world with 3,182 rooms, something that confirmed my observation that the Russians were fond of grandiosity. Less than two months before our visit a major fire broke out in a wing of the building killing 42 and injuring many more. One of the reasons for the high mortality rate was attributed to the hotel's dearth of exits, a purposeful design feature intended to make it difficult for guests to enter or exit unseen by hotel staff.

Every floor of every tourist hotel in Russia had its resident *babushka*, an elderly woman wearing a ubiquitous headscarf. In traditional Russian fashion, men wear hats; women scarves. The babushkas we came across grew up in hard times, many during the 1917 Revolution and then lived through the Great Patriotic War. They were generally tough, self-assured, loyal and respected.

Our appointed babushka sat behind a small table near the elevator with a samovar of hot water for tea at her side. She saw and reported on everyone who came and went, their time of arrival and moment of departure, communicating by phone or walkie talkie to the next agent who would follow us from the lobby. She, too, was a KGB informer, earning a few extra roubles per month to supplement her meagre state pension.

I don't remember ever seeing her smile. Not many people in Russia smiled, at least not in those days. It was a very serious country, still in the grip of a totalitarian government and only thirty years after World War II.

I later learned that there were other cultural reasons why Russians do not generally smile at strangers. Here are two excerpts from a revealing article discussing smiling in Russia:

> Russia is a collective culture, consisting of 'in-groups'. Russians do smile at people they know. Shop assistants smile at the clients they already know, not necessarily at others. If you smile at a stranger in Russia, he/she can smile back, but it can already mean an invitation to come and talk. Russians take smiling as a sign that the person cares about them. To smile at a stranger can raise the question: "Do we know each other?"
>
> You see two behaviours in one person in Russia: *Formal–unsmiling* is for 'them' (strangers); *friendly–smiling* for 'us' (friends, people we know). Some Russians skip to friendlier

Russian Jewish refuseniks demonstrating in front of the Ministry of Internal Affairs in Moscow for permission to emigrate from the USSR, while a KGB agent monitors the situation and prepares for their arrest. January 10, 1973.

behaviour after a shorter time. You can consider yourself accepted when people you have met begin smiling at you.[12]

It took me a while to fully appreciate the extent to which Russians lived under the shadow of the KGB.

KGB is the Russian-language abbreviation for Committee for State Security. It was the foreign intelligence and domestic security agency created in 1954 to serve as the "sword and shield of the Communist Party."

According to the *Encyclopedia Britannica*, the KGB was the largest secret-police and foreign-intelligence organization in the world with more than 480,000 personnel. Estimates of the number of informers in the Soviet Union itself were in the millions. They succeeded in infiltrating every major Western intelligence operation and in terrifying citizens at home. With the Communist Party and the army, the KGB formed the triad of power that ruled the Soviet Union until the fall of the USSR in 1991.

Clandestine humour is one coping mechanism for a population that has to deal with absurdity and oppression on a daily basis. Many years later, on a subsequent visit to St. Petersburg in the post-Communist era, our guide took us to the waterfront to visit the Russian cruiser *Aurora*. It was preserved as a museum ship, a proud symbol of the 1917 October Revolution. At the end of the tour, she pointed out a rather innocuous looking brick structure across the bay.

"See that building?" she asked, and then asserted, "It's the tallest in Russia."

It was only five storeys. She let us wait.

"It's the former headquarters of the KGB," she continued. "Even from its basement you could see Siberia!"

We soon discovered that the KGB controlled all the borders of a closed state that had isolated itself from the rest of the world. They were interested not just in who wanted to visit but also in who was trying to leave.

This directly impinged our lives immediately because the KGB wanted to be present anytime a Soviet citizen could come into contact with a foreigner. They knew every detail of our itinerary from landing to take-off including where we were staying and our planned tours.

Although Shmuel and I thought we were sometimes able to shake them off, we were probably mistaken. After all, they were the experienced ones; we were just rookie ravens. They stealthily tailed us when we went for walks, out for meals or took taxis to visit refuseniks. Cab drivers were obligated to report on the whereabouts of foreign travellers and all of our Intourist guides had been co-opted as part of their job description.

Intourist was the state-run travel monopoly set up to regulate the itinerary of foreign travellers including their flights to and from the country, travel restrictions within the country, where they could stay and eat, what they could see and who was licensed to guide them. Travel had to be a perfectly orchestrated experience in order to present the glory of the revolution in its best light.

But trouble was brewing in paradise.

Low productivity, inefficiency and a lack of innovation accentuated economic problems that resulted in a scarcity of food and consumer products. We were advised that two things some Russians might value were Levi jeans and ballpoint pens. We brought a few extra pairs of jeans and a handful of pens as gifts. They were distributed at appropriate times and were gratefully accepted. One recipient, a nonconformist rock musician, knew more about American music than I did. It was he who introduced me to the Doobie Brothers.

Some citizens, however, remained defensive about the Communist regime and championed statistics that purported to prove they were catching up to the industrial production of the West. They viewed it as an ideological Olympics that pitted Communism vs.

Capitalism. Shmuel and I were never very convincing when we tried to feign interest in the number of tons of steel produced and coal mined, in addition to advances in agriculture and manufacturing, all under Moscow's centralized series of Five Year Plans.

Only fifteen years later, on December 26, 1991, the red hammer & sickle flag would be lowered for the last time over the Kremlin. The grand, idealistic and bloody experiment of the Soviet Union would collapse under its own weight.

### Our Mission Begins

Once settled at the massive Rossiya Hotel in Moscow, my travelling companion and I communicated between ourselves through whispers, magic slates and hand signals as we uncovered our discreetly concealed contact list and made arrangements to meet with the first refuseniks.

### The Book of Photographs

A particularly memorable rendezvous was at the apartment of a teacher and his wife who had been trying to make *aliyah* [immigration to Israel is referred to as an "ascension," a "going up" both physically and spiritually to the Holy Land] to Israel for a number of years. In preparation for their hoped-for emigration they committed themselves to learning the Hebrew language through books. There was only one copy of a particular volume and they wanted to reproduce it so they could give additional copies to others in their learning circle.

Forbidden to print or import texts that the authorities deemed subversive, they were also not allowed to photocopy them at the library. The librarian—who, like countless others, reported to the KGB—had to approve the push of every button and she was not about to let grammar subvert the revolution. Consequently, the refuseniks and other dissidents created the *samizdat,* the underground self-publishing press, to produce their books.

After tea was served and trust established, the teacher led us to a small dark closet where he showed us their most recent pirated book of Hebrew grammar: It was a precarious stack of photographs—one photo per page—of the entire publication.

Over the next few days we managed to connect with other refuseniks in Moscow, always looking over our shoulders to see if we were being followed, a consequence that could endanger not just ourselves but also those who consented to meet with us.

### *Tea in Tajikistan*

Our Intourist guide drove us to the airport in Moscow and made sure that we got on our scheduled flight to our next destination. This was done as much out of kindness as out of an obligation to keep track of our whereabouts.

All flights to destinations within Russia were on Aeroflot, a state monopoly and the largest airline in the world. It was built out of a well-founded paranoia to serve the biggest country in the world, one that traversed eleven time zones. Domestic travel was heavily subsidized by the government in an effort to tie the colossal country together. At over 6,600,000 square miles it is almost twice the size of Canada or the United States.

Surreptitious visits with other persecuted individuals and families over the next ten days took us to Dushanbe in Tajikistan and then to Bukhara, Samarkand and Tashkent, all in Uzbekistan. All these destinations were on the ancient Silk Road connecting the East and the West. Our journey was scheduled to conclude with a return to Moscow for our flight across the Atlantic and back into the New World. We later discovered that some of our hosts had been questioned by the KGB for having dared meet with us; at least one was arrested. We were searched at each airport and some items were confiscated.

The next stop on our itinerary was a 1,860 mile flight to Dushanbe, the capital of Tajikistan, just north of the border with Afghanistan. It is on the northern segment of the ancient Silk Road trading route described by Marco Polo in the 13th century.

Jews first arrived in what is today Tajikistan in the 2nd century BCE. At the time of our visit the Jewish population of the country was approximately 15,000, mostly in Dushanbe. Today less than a few dozen remain, mostly elderly and poor who are also the target of antisemitic attacks.

Soon after arriving in Dushanbe we phoned our contact and were invited to come for a visit. The family of a father, mother and adult son didn't speak any English and we didn't know Russian or the local Tajik language so they invited a trusted non-Jewish friend to translate for us. We sat at their kitchen table and were served green tea (the national drink) and cookies. After about twenty minutes of confidence building and determining that we were who we claimed to be, we were offered some more tea, this time accompanied by a charming story with a window into local customs.

Before pouring the fresh tea into small handleless Tajik tea cups decorated with floral motifs, the father asked us if we noticed that the first cup was only filled half-way. The custom was to welcome everyone, friend or foe, and to extend hospitality with at least half a cup of tea. If the host didn't want the guest to stay, then the half-cup was drunk and the guest departed. But if the host liked you and wanted you to remain, then this time a full cup of welcoming hot brew was poured.

We remained for another couple of hours, sharing stories and exploits. Eventually a full meal was served accompanied by a homemade, bright green and very potent liquor. We drank a couple of glasses for lunch and they gifted us a bottle for the road.

### *Arrested as a Parasite; Absurdist humour*

Among the stories they shared with us was the recent fate of their eldest son. Accused of being a "Parasite of the Soviet State," i.e. living off the backs of others, he was arrested a month previously, given a multi-year sentence and was languishing in prison.

The bureaucratic reasoning for his arrest went something like this: 1) The Communist Soviet Union is a perfect entity; 2) it is dedicated to equality and is a workers' paradise; 3) there is no unemployment in such a state; 4) since you applied to emigrate, it is an indication that you no longer appreciate the country; 5) consequently, you were fired from your job; 6) since you are no longer working you are considered a parasite of the state; 7) parasites are traitors so you have been arrested and jailed.

The perfectly logical and yet blatantly absurd reasoning, backed by the power of the state, triumphed once again. I was reminded why gallows humour was a type of subtle social protest at a time when criticizing the government was forbidden and punishable by fines, imprisonment, disappearance or execution. Examples of such "labour humour" in the USSR include the following:

*Pretending*
"The authorities pretend they are paying wages; workers pretend they are working." Alternatively, "So long as the bosses pretend to pay us, we will pretend to work." Or, "We pretend to work and they pretend to pay."[13]

*Seven paradoxes of the socialist state*
Nobody works, but the plan is always fulfilled. The plan is fulfilled, but the shelves in the stores are empty. The shelves are empty, but nobody starves; nobody starves, but everybody is unhappy; everybody is unhappy, but nobody complains; nobody complains, but the jails are full.

### *Green liquor and intimidating strip search*

Our Dushanbe hosts had now become friends. They invited us to join them the next evening for the *seder* [traditional Passover ritual meal] on the First Night of *Pesah*. We brought them some of our Passover food. Our machine-manufactured Manischewitz matzah, however, paled in comparison to the handmade peasant unleavened bread that they were able to secure from a bootlegged Jewish source.

We recited the *Haggadah*, sang traditional songs and recounted the story of the Exodus from Egyptian slavery 3,500 years ago. Meanwhile, millions of embattled citizens in the USSR were in the midst of a modern-day exodus. History, as it often does, was repeating itself; we were witnesses to an unfolding story of biblical proportions.

As for vodka, the national alcoholic drink of Russia, we couldn't drink vodka fermented with cereal grains such as wheat or rye because of the prohibition against consuming *hamaitz* [leavened foods] on Passover. We did, however, find some intoxicating potato vodka that helped us to relax, celebrate with our hosts and temporarily forget the threatening forces looming just beyond the door.

But we had been followed. A couple of days after visiting the family in Dushanbe and celebrating Passover with them we arrived at the airport to fly to Bukhara, our next destination. The KGB-affiliated border guards had been tipped off, however, and were prepared to intimidate us. They conducted a thorough search of our luggage and bodies. Among the things they confiscated was the now precious bottle of green liquor, but I knew that duty-free shops at airports around the world were selling liquor and it was always being carried aboard airplanes.

"So why was it prohibited now?" I protested. One burly official opened the strong alcoholic drink and dramatically poured some of it over the back of the upholstered chair in front of us. He then reached in his pocket for a lighter, lit the alcohol, and pointed to the temporary flare-up like a proud pastry chef presenting a Baked Alaska flambé. He had decisively proven his point that it was flammable and dangerous to airline safety.

They then took Shmuel and me into separate rooms for interrogation to see if we would come up with the same stories as to where we were, who we visited and what was the real reason for our trip. They then conducted a strip search to humiliate us and to make sure we weren't trying to smuggle any other contraband out of Mother Russia.

Fortunately, they didn't uncover the list of contacts that our new friends gave us, nor did they find the names and numbers of our other contacts that had been furtively written in small letters in my now well-worn Arabian Nights. If they had discovered those names, phone numbers and addresses then all those refuseniks would have been re-arrested and subjected to further harassment, even imprisonment for conspiring with "foreign agents."

We were also informed that the people we'd visited in Dushanbe had been taken in for questioning and that they could be in further trouble for activities detrimental to the country.

Shaken by the interrogation but relieved at not having been arrested, we boarded the 44-seat twin propeller Antonov aircraft, code named "Coke" by NATO, and headed to our next destination an hour and a half away. Weather was poor; it was a tumultuous flight in the midst of a thunder storm and I feared that we'd never arrive alive. It would not be the first nor the last time that the Russian Secret Service had assassinated undesirables through alleged aviation mechanical failures. Fortunately we were not high profile enough to deal with in such a way; we were merely thorns in their collective sides.

### *Political satire*

Meanwhile, concerned for our host's safety and our role in exasperating their already tenuous situation, it was political satire that once again helped with gaining perspective:

*Freedom of speech*
Q: What is the difference between the Constitutions of the US and the USSR?
After all, both of them guarantee freedom of speech.
A: Yes, but the Constitution of the USA also guarantees freedom *after* the speech.

*Five precepts of the Soviet intelligentsia:*
- Don't think.
- If you think, then don't speak.
- If you think and speak, then don't write.
- If you think, speak and write, then don't sign.
- If you think, speak, write and sign, then don't be surprised.

*Propaganda*
Q: What should you do if a man you don't know takes a seat at your table in a pub and starts to sigh?
A: Immediately demand that he stops the anti-Soviet propaganda.

*Gulag inmates*
Three inmates in the Gulag corrective labour camps were telling one another what they were in for. The first one says "I was five minutes late for work and they charged me with sabotage." The second says "For me it was just the opposite: I was five minutes early for work and they charged me with espionage." The third one says "I got to work right on time and they charged me with harming the Soviet economy by acquiring a watch in a capitalist country."

*Soviet bureaucracy*
A man was ordered to come for a meeting at a government office to address some minor discrepancy. He was warned that if he did not attend to it immediately there would be severe consequences. He

called to make an appointment and after three days someone answered the phone. He was informed that the office was only open on the last Thursday of every month between the hours of 12 and 1 p.m. Upon arriving he noticed the name of the agency stencilled on the door— The Department of Redundancy Department. Under it, in large letters, was a sign that read: "Out to Lunch."

### Samarkand, Uzbekistan

Samarkand is an ancient 3,500-year-old Uzbek city variously described as the jewel or heart of the Silk Road stretching from China through India and Persia to the Mediterranean coasts of North Africa and Europe. Names associated with it include conquerors such as Alexander the Great, Genghis Khan and Tamerlane, the notorious Mongol-Turkish warrior who transformed Samarkand into one of the world's great cities. It has hosted a series of empires, civilizations and religions including Zoroastrian, Christian, Buddhist, Hindu, Manichaean and numerous other pagan spiritualities. With the Muslim conquest in the early 8$^{th}$ century it became an important centre for Islamic culture and scholarship. The famous Arab travel writer, Ibn Battuta, visited Samarkand in the early 1330s and described it as *"one of the greatest and finest of cities, and most perfect of them in beauty."*

Visiting Samarkand was like strolling through a waking dream. I was entranced by the rich blue and gold tiles intricately installed over soaring domes, all highlighted by chimerical latticework accentuated by honeycomb carvings into walls and ceilings decorated with non-representational art of florals, geometrics and Arabic calligraphy.

I remember the vast courtyards of mosques and madras schools where hundreds of students of the Koran used to sit and learn. Under Communist rule, however, religious institutions throughout the Soviet Union were mostly banned. Considered relics of the past and historically outdated curiosities, they were either repurposed or transformed into museums and related cultural sites.

The Russians were so convinced about the legitimacy, even the historical inevitability, of the Communist Revolution that although they were professed atheists they adopted the creed with an evangelical fervour. They were ardent believers in the cause and felt sanctioned justification for any purge within their own ranks or control of the general population as long as it served the long-range goals of the Party. Tragically, more people were killed as a result of international Communist policies than even under the murderous Fascists. Here is another example of the "people's humour" to counteract such self-righteous bravado:

*The Revolution and Strawberry Ice Cream*
In the days leading up to the Bolshevik Revolution a Party leader was haranguing the crowd assembled in front of the Kremlin.

"Come the Revolution," he declared, "everyone will have strawberry ice cream!"

To which everyone cheered except for one little girl standing at the back who put up her hand and meekly protested, "But I don't like strawberry ice cream."

To which he responded, "Come the Revolution you *will* like strawberry ice cream!"

Samarkand was also home to vibrant markets selling all kinds of manufactured goods and food products. Under Communist central planning most of the produce had to be turned over to the government which then sold it. This resulted in a loss of personal incentive and a significant shortage of food. At the time of our visit, agricultural economic reforms had recently been introduced allowing farmers to keep 20% of their own produce and sell it for a profit. This resulted in positive consequences that stimulated productivity, the economy and personal satisfaction.

Shmuel and I were not originally scheduled to visit Samarkand and were not given any refuseniks to contact there. I lobbied for it to be included on our itinerary based on a LIFE magazine article that I'd read ten years previously. In March 1967, LIFE reported on then-Vice President Richard Nixon's visit to the Soviet Union. It included a stopover in Samarkand with a multi-page full-colour spread of photographs depicting the intriguing blue-tiled, high-domed, centuries-old mosques that transformed it for me into a fantasy scene out of the Seven Voyages of Sinbad. I was transported into magical realms of supernatural adventure leading to fortune by fate. The still-anonymous organization that sponsored our expedition eventually relented and, as a favour to our intrepid duo, squeezed it in between our other focused destinations.

By an act of synchronicity, I later discovered that Samarkand was also mentioned in the exploits of Scheherazade, the beautiful vizier's daughter and wise storyteller who remained alive by telling stories to the king for 1001 nights. It was a fortuitous coincidence that a copy of the classic narrative accompanied me on this exotic voyage and protected the identity of our refusenik contacts within the deep gutter of its paperback pages.

### Bukhara—the most mysterious city

Bukhara, described as "the most mysterious city of the silk road," was the scene of our next hoped-for meetings. Our Intourist guide picked us up at the airport, checked us in to the hotel and gave us a tour of the city. Every guide was instructed to promote the accomplishments of the Revolution so we were taken to carefully considered sites. I remember being somewhat disappointed at first because we were just shown factories and housing projects. I was reminded of Be'er Sheva in Israel, a location mentioned in the bible but today a modern town at the north end of the Negev Desert. I was hoping to experience the exotic bazaars filled with carpet and spice merchants of the rumoured Bukhara of long-ago. After touring a series of new developments we were finally introduced to the Old Town with its mosques, minarets, madrasas, a large fortress, impressive citadel and the old market under the Four Domes.

Jewish life in Bukhara is reputed to stretch back 3,000 years to the time of King David when Israelite traders traveled to Central Asia. Local tradition claims the Bukharian Jews were part of the ten Lost Tribes, specifically Naftali and Yissahar. Numerous other mentions are made in various historical texts, including the Talmud, that locate Jewish communities in the region. Once Tamerlane conquered the area, he brought Jews from Persia to bolster trade and help revitalize the then-abandoned Silk Road. Cultural fortunes ebbed and flowed during the ensuing centuries until there was a resurgence in the late 1700s. Throughout the next two centuries thousands of Bukharian Jews emigrated to Jerusalem where they established the fabled Bukharian Quarter.

One of the leaders of the Bukharian community in Jerusalem was Rabbi Shlomo Moussaieff (1852–1922). He described his motivation for moving to Israel in the following words [translated from the Hebrew]:

> I, Shlomo Moussaieff, am a native of Bukhara. My spirit moved me to leave the land of my birth, in which I grew up, and to ascend to the Holy Land, the land in which our ancestors dwelled in happiness, the land whose memory passes before us ten times each day in our prayers. ... We do not have any festive occasion without a mention of Jerusalem. ... There is no doubt that I am required to thank God for all the good He has done for me. He has brought me across the sea three times. He has kept me alive, and has brought me to the place of my desire for good life and peace to see the pleasantness of God and to visit His sanctuary. ...

Shlomo (Suleiman) Yekutieli, a friend who was raised in the venerable community of Herat, Afghanistan, once related a fascinating anecdote about Jewish settlement along the bygone Silk Route. The Jewish people were instructed by the Torah to work for six days but to then rest on the seventh, the Sabbath (Shabbat). This commandment laid the foundations of a rhythm for Jewish merchants: They travelled by donkey, horse, camel, by boat (when there were waterways) or on foot for six days but stopped at the nearest town before the seventh in honour of the Sabbath. That is where Jewish communities sprang up and why they were spaced six travel days apart.

### *Tashkent—a city of refuge*

Tashkent, the capital of Uzbekistan, was another major trading centre along the Silk Road and has remained a significant exporter of textiles, especially to Eastern Europe. While there I was introduced to Ikat, the most renowned of Uzbek textiles that are hand dyed and woven on traditional handlooms using a resist-dyeing method. I fell in love with the colourful material and purchased a number of items including a bolt of cloth for future use.

We only visited one refusenik family in Tashkent and experienced no major difficulties. Hopefully we were able to encourage and reassure them that many people outside of the restrictive USSR were doing everything in their power to assist with their impending emigration.

The history of the Jews in Uzbekistan refers to the history of two distinct communities: the more religious and traditional Bukharian community and the European Ashkenazi community. During WWII, more than one million Jewish refugees from Nazi-occupied eastern Europe passed through Uzbekistan. Many remained there, especially in Tashkent, after the war and a large Jewish settlement was thus created. There were 103,000 Jews in Uzbekistan in 1970; less than 10,000 remained in 2021 (3,700 in Tashkent).

## *Incarnation of the Original Sin*

Upon the completion of our mission to Central Asia, Shmuel and I flew back to Moscow from where we would catch our return flight through Frankfurt to New York's John F. Kennedy International Airport. President Kennedy was another victim of the Cold War, having been assassinated in 1963 by Lee Harvey Oswald who was implicated for his connections with both the Soviet Union and Cuba.

The near-psychosis that we experienced in those days was palpable, fuelled by the imminent threat of a nuclear war that could end life on earth at the press of a button. Deterrence was only tenuously achieved through "Mutual Assured Destruction" (MAD), a "theory that assumed that each superpower had enough nuclear weaponry to destroy the other. If one superpower attempted a first strike on the other, they themselves would also be destroyed."[14]

Cold War paranoia also seized the West, especially America. It was the time of the Red Scare featuring the McCarthy Witch Hunts. Every good citizen was encouraged to report suspicious activity to the authorities. Similar to the USSR, street-level humour helped to diffuse tension in America, the ultimate spoof coming from the 1962 song "The John Birch Society" by the Chad Mitchell Trio. The song's memorable punch line was "If mommie is a commie then you gotta turn her in."

I remember our last night in Moscow. Gazing out the darkened window in our monitored hotel room I contemplated what it was like living in a police state, in perpetual fear and under constant surveillance. I was awake but still felt trapped in a nightmare in which I—and all those confined in the murky Xenophobic Utopia—was a criminal guilty of some amorphous, never-ending violation.

It felt as if everyone was guilty of something even if they didn't quite know what it was. The Revolution was the new god and each one of us was an incarnation of the original sin, not necessarily for something we had already transgressed but for something that we *might* do. We were guilty just because we existed.

### We are all spies

As midnight in Moscow deepened into a sleepless reverie, I concluded that we were all spies—our five senses acting as stalwart agents gathering information that might give us some advantage in the competitive parade of life. Everything that exists is involved in the surveillance of other entities that might prove to be either a threat or a benefit. Espionage inhabits a sliding scale stretching from subatomic particles to the universe itself. On a personal level, the information gleaned from our environment influences our choice of friends, shapes our thoughts and warns us of potential dangers. On a national scale, spying on other countries results in a series of allies or enemies, peace agreements or defensive military pacts, economic sanctions or declarations of war. Do the skies not watch over the earth even as scarred terrain undermines the vault of heaven?

It took a couple of months to readjust to Western culture—to its relative freedom, open architecture and unfettered economy. I was astonished at fully stocked food stores, neon lights, traffic jams, advertising and uncensored art. It was as if I was swimming in an ocean of freedom instead of drowning in a whirlpool of fear. But the PTSD took time to dissipate: I felt a tinge of panic every time I saw a policeman and wasn't sure if I could ever trust another person again for fear they would report my subversive thoughts and turn me in.

### Mystery Solved

After writing a report for the mystery organization that organized our exploit, Shmuel and I returned to civilian life and our eighteen-hour days of study. I never spoke about the operation again. Until now.

For thirty years I didn't know what secret counter-intelligence administration recruited us, planned the trip and sent us on our overseas mission. We were advised not to ask too many questions.

The answer finally appeared in a front-page story on October 26, 2007 in the *Jewish Independent*. The headline announced "Nativ's new mission: Old organization has new objectives," by Gil Zohar. The article reported on what was now declassified information but I was surprised to see it in print in the public domain. Instinctively self-protective, I felt betrayed. It read:

> The semi-covert immigration encouragement organization *Lishkat Hakesher* (the Liaison Bureau), code-named *Nativ* (Hebrew for path), maintained contact with Jews living in the Eastern Bloc during the Cold War and encouraged immigration to Israel. *Nativ* served as a liaison for *refuseniks*—Jewish dissidents in the Soviet Union—and has played a key role in the immigration of 1.5 million Jews to Israel over the last six decades. ... In the mid-1970s, international pressure forced the Soviet Union to allow greater emigration, and the number of Soviet Jews leaving for Israel increased dramatically. The collapse of the Soviet Union in 1991 ended the need to conduct operations clandestinely.

Shmuel and I were never going to be protagonists for a John le Carré novel but at least now our secret was out. During our short-lived espionage careers we had been taken to school by what sometimes felt like scenes out of Mad Magazine's *Spy vs. Spy* feature cartoon. We were the black-hatted, Talmud-toting Paladin Brothers: *Have Spy – Will Travel*. We both ended up in education.

Without humour, what's a "meta for"?[15] So, to make sense of everything, let us conclude with a distinctly Russian joke:

## A Visit from the KGB

Back in the darkest days of the Soviet Union, a KGB agent goes into a ratty old building.

He walks up several flights of stairs and knocks on the door of a dingy apartment with a name plate that says DAVIDOVICH.

No one answers so the agent pounds on the door again until finally an old man in a shabby coat appears.

"Does the tailor Davidovich live here?"

"No."

"Who are you?"

"Davidovich."

"So why did you say Davidovich doesn't live here?"

"You call this living?"

The last time I saw my partner in crime, Shmuel, was a few years after our Soviet caper. He was living in Tsfat (Safed), an esteemed town of mystics, artists and poets, the highest municipality in the Galilee and in all of Israel. He had moved there with his wife and was teaching elementary school children. He seemed genuinely happy when he told me that there was nothing better than teaching Grade Three students. At the time I found it hard to believe. Now I don't.

I sometimes wish that I was that age again, eight or nine years old, protected by my elders and teachers, on the cusp of wonder. Being an adult has been filled with opportunity but it has also been a much more difficult venture, one threatened with persecution and challenges as I continue to search for peace and freedom in what used to be such a promising new world.

# NEW LIFE JOKE SHOP

"Joke Shop is the world." Welcome to a confectionery, a philosophical variety store, a word emporium of observations on Ageing, Art, Books, Charity, City, Collecting, Conflict, Criticism, Death, Design, Desire, Gardens, Genius, Happiness, Holocaust, Imperfection, Knowledge, Libraries, Museums, Nazis, Peace, Pilgrimage, Poetry, Presentations, Psyche, Psychogeography, Quest, Story, Technology, War, Work.

## ON AGEING

I continue to fly through the world on elder wings; still able to get off the ground but humbled by the gravities within.

## ON ART

Art is a living, dynamic force that can be harnessed both for creation and destruction, for blessing and a curse, for good or for evil. Art is the eternal heart ever-beating within the creative soul. We, ourselves, are living art, the sensate product of a supremely prolific universe.

In time before time—deep in the spaceless presence of Infinite Silence—something stirred. It was an intimation of the Universal Will to experience manifest matter. As an artisan acquiring her trade, the Empyreal Architect created and destroyed many worlds, considered and rejected numerous plans, before finally declaring *ki tov,* that this, our world, was good.[16]

During those early attempts to generate reality, only mind and measure, logic and law, were used in the divine equation. These techniques alone proved to be too severe, causing those prototypical models to shatter into mirrored grains of luminous dust. It was only when heart complimented head, and mercy attenuated judgment, that the world stood momentarily still and the Genius of Art was called forth, appointed to oversee the creative tension of Natural Law.[17]

The search for the Source of Creation is not for the faint of heart. Art is beast as much as beauty, madness more than tranquility, mind as much as matter and dedicated labour more than blissful contemplation. Art can be made to serve many masters yet ultimately it can never be tamed.

Art is an aspect of the *anima mundi* (World Soul). It offers itself as a fertile field for the germination of the Celestial Seed scattered by the winds of desire. Beauty excites our passions not just for the sake of secret pleasure but also as a trusted agent of the biological imperative for survival. Often, it is Art that is immutable and we who are transient; it is Art that creates and we who must obey.

Art is both Eden's paradise as well as her subtle serpent urging us to ingest the alluring centre—it was "a delight to the eyes"—convincing us that "on the day that you eat of it then your eyes shall be opened and you shall be as gods."[18] It was Art that committed the original sin.

To the discerning eye, all is transparent. What appears on the surface to be divergent phenomena are actually just a series of transliterations, each one a recapitulation of the singular Essence. Perhaps Emerson expressed it best when he wrote:

> Herein is the explanation of the analogies which exist in all the arts. They are the reappearance of one mind, working in many materials to many temporary ends. Raphael paints wisdom, Handel sings it, Phidias carves it, Shakespeare writes it, Wren builds it, Columbus sails it, Luther preaches it, Washington arms it, Watt mechanizes it [...]. The laws of each art are convertible into the laws of every other.[19]

The cosmos is drenched, thoroughly permeated with art as principle, material and as active being appearing in the guise of seemingly neverending incarnations. Art can be simple, art can be kind: it is gentle, constructive and comforting. It can also be a precise tyrant, brutally exacting and cruelly judgmental. Were it not for borders and boundaries, however, beauty itself would disappear.

Wrestling with Reality, we become real. That is the essence of art.

*Excerpts from Reflections on Art & the Artist, a speech that the author delivered upon receiving an honorary doctorate from Emily Carr University of Art + Design, Vancouver, May 8, 2004. The text, with an Introduction by Dr. Ron Burnett and designed by Robert R. Reid, was published in a limited edition by Aryel Publishing House. — Ed.*

Shakespeare and Company Bookstore, Paris. Photo by Cynthia Copper-Benjamin

## ON BOOKS
*The well-designed book*

A generic book could be simply described as a set of written, printed or blank pages fastened along one side and encased between protective covers. But the well-designed, limited edition or rare book is another species altogether for it is also concerned with the quality, uniqueness and aesthetic value of each volume. Not only are the words themselves important, but extra care is also paid to the book's edition, quality of content, design, printing and provenance.

It is not sufficient that words alone be legible. Additional dimensions are brought to bear, ones that appreciate (with a sense of exquisite attention borne upon the winds of infinite patience) the potion of ink, the vintage of press and the mill of paper. We lift the book to the light as well as to the shadow to catch the glint upon the ink, as fresh today as it was five hundred years ago. We notice the paper's thickness, its alluring texture, and its amorous receptivity to impression as if making love with the mechanical printing press.

Just as human hair is transformed with age to a crown of silver, so, too, a fine folio develops an ivory-coloured coat gracefully matured in the crucible of time.

The fairest books are fastened with sewing skill and then draped with linens and leathers worthy of *haute couture*. Such great consideration is lavished upon the binding that even an accidental glance can result in a profound aesthetic experience that at once quickens the eye and captures the heart.

Who can resist, as if by personal invitation, reaching out to raise the book, to know its weight and absorb its well-earned reputation. Fragrance, along with history, is inhaled in a swift osmotic migration from the master's depths to the bibliophile's longing for completion.

The most magnificent books achieve that rare combination of outer vision with inner content. It is something that we, in our complex psychospiritual unfolding, spend a lifetime growing towards. Contrary to popular proverb, when happening upon such publications one could very well "judge a book by its cover."

Design is not just an afterthought or a minor detail; it is not an inconvenience nor a stumbling block. Design is wings and wonder; it is a reliquary, an appropriate vessel—grand or humble, heavy or thin—for all those who would be embraced by its protective aesthetics. The slimmest volume attired in time and texture, in exquisitely composed space and perfect typeface, is a parenthetical reiteration of Creation itself. Since we cannot achieve perfection in ourselves, we can at least attempt it in our works.

When we gaze upon this fine book or that bold building, when we hear music that animates the soul, when we garb our bodies in impeccable textiles designed by a master tailor, or taste a sublime recipe that closes the eyes and awakens the flavours of Eden—these works serve as a mentoring mirror to arouse us, once again, to the highest calling of the possible human. This is true for every encounter with the noble arts.[20]

The well-designed book, therefore, is not only beautiful, it is also necessary. Each particular tome, the singular book before me, echoes the macrocosmic Book of Being whose pages are the heavens, quills the forests and whose inks are scooped from the hypnotic seas. It is a Book whose content squeezes past its straining covers, a binding that simply cannot contain the eternal parade that marches beyond the borders of any known world.

There are times, however, when material aesthetics pale in the presence of moral propriety and basic needs. This was the experience of the 17th century Japanese Zen master, Tetsugen, as he attempted to print the Buddhist sutras newly translated from the Chinese.

The books were to be printed with carved wood blocks in an edition of seven thousand copies, an enormous undertaking. To cover expenses, Tetsugen travelled throughout the country collecting donations. Some benefactors contributed greatly to the cause but most of the time he received only a few coins. He thanked each donor with equal gratitude.

After ten years Tetsugen had enough money to begin his task. Just at that time, however, the Uji River overflowed. Famine followed so Tetsugen took the funds he had collected for the book and spent them to save others from starvation.

Once again, he began raising money to prepare for printing the sacred verses. Several years passed and he was almost ready to begin his dream project when an epidemic spread throughout the country. Without hesitation, Tetsugen gave away what he had collected in order to help his people.

For a third time he started his work, and after twenty years his wish was fulfilled. The printing blocks which produced that first edition of *sutras* can be seen today in the Obaku monastery in Kyoto. The Japanese tell their children that Tetsugen made three sets of *sutras*, and that the first two surpass even the last.[21]

*Dedicated to Robert Bringhurst, Robert R. Reid, Paul Whitney, Ralph Stanton and Ann Cowen, friends in the book.*

## ON CHARITY

There is no greater charitable act than becoming a friend to someone in need.

> Everyone knows that in Jerusalem every beggar has his own street corner.
> 
> A man who used to pass by a particular corner always gave something to the beggar.

One day, as he reached in his pocket for change, he realized he didn't have any money.

"I'm sorry, my friend, but I don't have anything to give you today."

The beggar laughed and danced, to which the man repeated:

"No, no. Perhaps you misunderstood. I'm sorry but I have nothing to give."

"Yes, I know," replied the beggar, "but you called me your friend."

The Torah insists that we be proactive and creative in our giving, that we turn it into an art, that we chase after opportunities to assist with all our hearts, with all our souls and with all our might. We come to realize, along with Rav Yisrael Salanter, that "the *physical* needs of the other are my *spiritual* needs" and that my spirituality is most fulfilled not on the mountaintop but beside those who need me. Nurturing others, we come to realize that they are just us in disguise.

We do not turn away from the poor who are wrapped in worry, finding refuge only in sleep; we don't neglect the homeless who wander from shelter to street, nor do we forsake the unemployed who search desperately for dignity. We do not abandon the abused who must fend off beating and rape, or the children who bear scars on their bodies and trauma in their souls.

It is with empathy that we embrace the immigrant mind. We know their hearts because we, too, were strangers. ("There is nothing more whole than a broken heart," sighed Levi Yits'hak of Berditchev, for when something breaks it is opened wider than ever before.) We are also there with those who suffer from chronic mental illness, those who cannot make sense of what we call "normal," and who must absorb curious looks and cruel remarks. We know they struggle, laugh and cry as we do. Only more so.

Giving of our resources, or of our time, is both a privilege and a discipline. It can also be a terrible burden. No individual, or even entire governments, can completely eradicate poverty, pain and suffering. Even if we gave everything we have, it would still not be sufficient. Although we may not be able to fulfill everyone's needs we can at least begin the task—one cent and one second at a time.

This compassionate work cannot just be relegated to professionals. It is also our responsibility, those of us who would dare to stumble and stutter in the dust, for the lower we stoop the taller we stand. This is the true meaning of charity, of *tzedakah*: it is simply doing the right thing at the right time with the right attitude. A simple act of kindness done with sincere intentions is equal to all the other commandments combined. It does not have to be elegant and it does not have to be large but it does have to be.

Even if everyone else has disappeared, will we be the ones who reach out in friendship, who respond *Hineini*, "Here I am"? Even if we can't, we can. It is the highest social-spiritual accomplishment one can attain.

*Excerpts from YW's "The One Friend Who Was Needed to Mend a Broken Heart," an inspirational address at the Jewish Family Service Agency's Innovators Luncheon, Hyatt Regency Hotel, Vancouver, on May 17, 2007. Keynote speaker was Craig Newmark, founder of Craigslist. — Ed.*

## ON CITY

A city is not just an amalgamation of buildings but also a social contract wherein a large number of people agree to live relatively close to one another. The price we pay is giving up some of our freedoms in exchange for other mutual benefits such as culture, law enforcement, infrastructure, education, health and social services. In the very act of abdicating our individual freedoms, however, civilization fills us with discontents, for we resent—consciously or unconsciously—having been so domesticated.

The metropolitan fair is occupied by more than just humans adorned in the robes of their constant drama. We may be a poem of our city, defined by the parenthesis of mountain and sea; we may be wandering pilgrims and humble hermits, thieves and lovers among the woods and waters of Lotus Land, but we are only *one* species, a minority in the midst of many.

Remember the moss and the mushroom thriving in lavish rainforest where each drop is a diamond and morning-dew a jewel of the resurrected dawn. Ours is a Garden City—every garden has its rose; each rose its thorn. The city is a living organism; the atmosphere dynamically charged. Let us celebrate our urban oasis and embrace its astonishing diversity as an archetypal ambassador of all that exists.

*Excerpt from YW's speech upon being presented with the Freedom of the City award by the City of Vancouver, May 30, 2022. — Ed.*

## ON COLLECTING

Collecting is a natural phenomenon. To collect well, however, requires extraordinary effort. The sun collects planets and constellations their stars while the oceans gather their many waters. Humans never tire of their cornucopian collections: it is our fate to make order out of constant cosmic momentum, to domesticate chaos in the crucible of mind, to embrace infinity through the transcendent lens of a restless soul and to be held hostage by our emotions whether of unforgiving pain or the mixed pleasures of life's daily drama.

Originally, we collected to survive—food for sustenance, fuel for warmth, land for living and stories for identity. Collecting then became somewhat of a luxury, humble or ostentatious, when it was used for power, entertainment, wealth and aesthetics.

Collecting may be a patient, lifelong endeavour and serve many purposes, but at a certain point one can finally release the accumulated cache and relax into accepting things as they are. One day, we, too, will be collected by the Earth and scattered—along with our possessions—as dust in the evening wind. The universe is the greatest collector of all; we are merely local incarnations. Each galaxy is a gallery; every atom a work of art.

## ON CONFLICT

Conflict is inherent in human consciousness. In the heavens themselves. If not for conflict, reality as we know it would not exist.

Except for the transcendent Principle of Unity—the singular, undifferentiated Essence from which everything emanates—all that exists, with few exceptions, seems to partake of a series of dualities: up over down, left implies right, north suggests south, male relates to female, kinetic emerges from potential, hot is on a spectrum with cold, good opposes evil, light separated from darkness and winning triumphs over defeat. There are copious other examples including Newton's Third Law of Motion that states "for every action there is an equal and opposite reaction."

Every world religion and secular philosophy had to deal with the issue of dualistic conflict including the venerable Chinese philosophy of *Yin* and *Yang* and the ancient Persian religion of Zoroastrianism.[22] Other religions were based not on monotheism or theistic dualism but rather on polytheism—a plethora of competing deities. Even those religions that believe in monotheism, one god, still have to deal with traits of both metaphysical and ethical dualism.

Questions arise such as "If there is only one God, can it be simultaneously credited as not only the source of creation and all that is good, but also with death, decay, suffering and evil?"[23]

It seems that although the idea of a singular *source* of reality is introduced—e.g. one God or a Unified Field Theory—reality itself always manifests in at least a duality, and more often a multiplicity, of competing forces. The closest we can get to describing the original undifferentiated Source, is to use awkward, suggestive, symbolic language. Every civilization and their most brilliant minds have wrestled with the mystery of conflict. Many responses have been elicited—some elegant, others awkward, all theoretical—but the Original Question remains.

Conflict and confusion—remnants of the original chaos of creation—continue to exist, even if they were wounded when forced to make room for order. Some say this cosmic choreography will always be with us. Others suggest that just as conflicted duality emerged from Undifferentiated Spirit, so, too, matter and related forces will complete their cycle of existence some day and return to their source.

In the meantime, our complex *Homo sapiens* mind continues to dwell simultaneously in many dimensions: we are aware of being aware of being aware. That is the cause, most often, of emotional, intellectual and moral pain for we live in a hall of conflicting mirrors. We tend to react to every rule we make and transgress as often as we fulfill.

### *Why sports are so popular*

The underlying principles of conflict are also why sports are so popular. Not only are we born into vast competitions and learn to participate in pre-existing social tournaments, but we also create rules of our own making in a series of self-imposed games. It is a way of actualizing story, of activating narrative, our principal modus operandi through which we make sense of phenomena and communicate it to others.

Athletics are a subset of conflict, something that we rather apologetically label not as *conflict* but as *competition*. They are a socially accepted, pre-arranged series of "games." We disguise conflict by dressing it in uniforms, splashing it with proprietary colours, and by assigning names, numbers and totems such as the Eagles, Bears, Lions and the Sharks.

Sports are a metaphor for conflict; a surrogate for war. They are a competition between opposing forces [teams] as exemplified by ego identity. Personal ego identity telescopes from the personal to the universal. Me against you expands into my team against your team and then my city or country versus another. It reflects the classic tension between the individual and the world.

When my team is victorious, it means that I, too, am a winner. The Life Force that animates us is behind even that personal sentiment. To the victor goes the spoils. Winning means that my species survives, that it thrives, that we are the Chosen One. To the unconscious, even a friendly neighbourhood game is a grand tournament between *Eros* and *Thanatos,* life and death incarnate.

We have learned that it is far better to organize athletic competitions than to actually hunt one another; that it is preferable to challenge each other, or to test our own limits, than it is to unilaterally destroy the other. Instead of hurling munitions at one another, it is mutually advantageous to kick, bat, throw or hit a ball between us.

Conflict takes many forms. It is opposition, a thwarting of desire, disagreement and incompatibility. It exists within the self, between two or more individuals, between groups, ideas, organizations or the series of mechanical forces that constitute reality. It can lead to friction, violence, destruction or to balance and resolution.

Not all conflict is bad, inappropriate or destructive. Some is creative, natural, entertaining, inevitable and beneficial. The root of the English word derives from the Latin, *con + fligere,* "to strike together." Striking two things together most often results in assault and injury. It could, however, also produce a meeting of shared minds, a blending of complimentary forces or a spark leading to a passionate union.

Gravity, magnetism and nuclear forces remain captive to the intractable laws of nature and must obey their dictates. Others, however, don't always play by the rules. It is they who can, on rare occasions, transcend the game and bring resolution to conflict. This was exemplified by an occurrence at the 1976 Special Olympics:

> Nine contestants lined up at the starting line for the 100 yard dash. At the sound of the gun, they all took off as best they could. One young boy, however, stumbled, tumbled to the ground and began to cry. Hearing his cries, two of the other racers slowed down and looked back. Then without hesitation, they turned around and began running in the other direction.
>
> While the rest of the contestants struggled to complete the race, the two who had turned around reached for the boy and helped him to his feet. All three of them linked arms and together they walked to the finish line. By the time the trio reached the end, everyone in the stadium was standing and cheering, many in tears. Even though by turning back they lost their own chance to win, they all had smiles on their faces knowing they did the right thing.

## ON CRITICISM

Most people resent criticism. However, creative criticism is an act of generosity. It helps to improve both the form and content of the art, the person or the phenomenon being critiqued. It adds a dimension of creative tension and a breath of perspective.

Not all know how to criticize, fewer understand how to accept it, but ultimately everyone benefits.

Being the recipient of criticism is even more difficult than being the critic. We are all trying to survive and when threatened—whether by nature, personal doubt or a considered enemy—we respond in complex ways.[24]

What the artist sometimes forgets is that cultural criticism is not the same as moral rebuke. It is not bullying nor an exercise in public shaming but rather a gift and a challenge.[25] Anyone can use criticism as a weapon, but only the mature critic wields his pen like a skilled surgeon and her words as a healing balm.

On the other hand, the one being critiqued does not have to accept the review. After all, it is only someone else's opinion, and the playwright could declare with the inimitable Oscar Wilde: "The play was a great success but the audience was a total failure."

Effective criticism is as remarkable as it is rare: it reminds us of the Ideal when the mundane doesn't live up to its potential. Its light scatters shadows[26] and awakens the reader to an expanded sense of reality. The critic must have the courage to see what exists and speak its name but should not seek to humiliate the one being critiqued. The artist and the critic complement one another: one acts, the other reacts; one sounds, the other echoes; one offers, the other receives; one is a servant, the other a slave.

The critic is part of a vast *cultural ecology*. The authentic critic does not offer a critique to stand apart from the art or artist—although detached objectivity is imperative. Creative criticism is humble, not arrogant. It may be confident, daring and bold but ultimately it remains subservient to art and culture.

The highest calling of the critic is as a force of nature, to serve as a mentor, and, if permitted, as a co-creator. Constructive criticism is an indication that the critic, whether writer or broadcaster, is aware that she is a cell of a larger organism who has regard for both the artist's struggles and achievements. Criticism is not always harsh.

The critic evaluates better than most of us, for we are too diffident to reveal the thing as it is in itself—*das Ding an sich*. We tend to become apologists for mediocrity.

We often subjugate our warrior eye to a timid heart, exchange cultured taste for manufactured irrelevance, refute the Music of the Spheres for a cacophony of urban noise and sacrifice perfection in the name of compromise. Without critics to charge us, we gravitate to lower standards and become like false idols that have mouths but cannot speak and eyes but cannot see.[27]

Critics, however, are not afraid of expressing themselves. As one who is both blessed and burdened with a multisensory palette of impressions, the cultural commentator partakes of acute observation and exquisite discernment. He is an objective ambassador—beholden to no one—who stands between the art and the public, a representative of both artist and audience. She must be able to see clearly, listen intensely, imagine prophetically and render reviews with the animated authority of a judge called to sit on the bench of Public Perception.

The critic also fulfills another role—that of cheerleader and champion, one who reports ovations, thrills and transcendent triumph. In its finest expression, cultural criticism is as noble an art as the craft itself.

*YW created a province-wide award, the Max Wyman Award for Critical Writing, named in honour of former Vancouver Sun arts columnist and critic Max Wyman, O.C., D.Litt. (hon). – Ed.*

## ON DEATH

It has been a modest privilege
to explore every continent
and sail the seven seas.

The final note
in the concluding octave
of conceivable scenarios
is now the focus
of what remains
of this earthly sojourn
before I'm reluctantly recalled
to fertilize the garden
with the remnants
of my broken body
and disappearing soul,
the same patched plot
I once cultivated so carefully.

I've already passed
my best before date
yet still trust
my diminishing itinerary
might reveal itself
with the unexpected sweetness
of a warm summer rain.

## ON DESIGN

*In the midst of eternity, designers dress the universe.*

Art inhabits a continuum from the dawn of creation to the very end of time. Design is evident not just in the visual and plastic arts but also in the more subtle technologies of song and dance, the shape of thought, the embrace of emotions and the theologies of spiritual transcendence.

Design saturates the world from fashion to architecture and from ephemeral graphics to heavy industry. Designers even engage in prophecy for they must intuit future taste—at times even dictate it—until yesterday's unknown becomes tomorrow's must-have.

Humanity, however, should not arrogate the phenomenon of design to ourselves. It began long before the advent of our species. Design is a celestial principle: we are merely its regional emissaries.

We exist within a Grand Sequence which was forged through thousands of forces that conspired to sculpt the planets and roll the waves, that blow the winds and sparkle the stars. The forces of gravity and magnetism, fire, water, earth and air are among the experienced hands that shape material reality. The plant and animal worlds—from ancient Trees of Life to bearded lions, schools of fish and soaring birds—have also adapted to the forces that form and decorate them. The world is attired in nothing but art and design, for these principles have permeated every aspect of existence.

Beauty is a guiding principle for some and a natural result for others. Buckminster Fuller (1895–1983) echoed this sentiment when he observed, "When I am working on a problem I never think about beauty but when I have finished, if the solution is not beautiful, I know it is wrong." And it was Baldassare Castiglione, in his 1528 *Il Libro del Cortegiano,* who declared, "No matter what things you study, you will always find that those which are good and useful are also graced with beauty."

The world is a better place because of designers, their care and dedication to their craft. They are cultural heroes to whom we are forever indebted.

*YW was the longtime patron of the Carter Wosk Awards for Applied Art & Design established by the British Columbia Achievement Foundation. Considered the most prestigious recognition in the province for applied arts and design, the awards celebrate those, who through their creativity, contribute to the cultural and economic fabric of the community. – Ed.*

## ON DESIRE

Buddhists warn of desire as the root of suffering. Desire does not just infect humanity but rather all existence is implicated in its insatiable yearning for a series of goals. The extent of human desire, however, exceeds them all.

I, too, have been caught in the web of wanting more. Learning more. Feeling, understanding and accomplishing more. Immortality, pleasure, love and health; power, wealth, honour and humility. These desires, even in the presence of one's best intentions, can turn ominous, just as the deepest darkness dwells in the shadow of the brightest light.

But it is this impatient inclination for wanting to experience the omniscient Mind of Genesis that motivates us to more fully partake in the ever-evolving cosmos. As my teacher, the Catholic theologian Thomas Berry, once articulated: *"We are the earth made conscious of itself."*

We may have accomplished many things but relative to eternity it is as if we never even existed. Instead of falling into existential despair, however, it is better to believe that everything, even the most extraordinary, is possible.

That is my desire.

## ON GARDENS

*For a person is a tree of the field.*
*Deut. 20:19*

*Trees are the earth's endless effort to speak to the listening heaven.*
— Rabindranath Tagore

### The Wisdom of a Cherry Tree

In a forest, each being depends upon and provides for others. The blossoms of a cherry tree bring forth a new generation of cherry trees, while also providing food for micro-organisms which renew the soil and support the growth of further plant-life.

> Like a cherry tree, humans are a part of nature. To thrive and prosper in a modern world, we have to design our buildings like trees, and our cities like forests.
> — *From architect Bing Thom's "The Shanghai Principles"*

### A 2,000-Year-Old Talmudic Tree Tale

One day Honi was walking along a road and saw a man planting a carob tree.
He asked him: "How long does it take to bear fruit?"
"Seventy years," the man replied.
The sage then asked him: "Are you certain you will live another seventy years?"
To which the man answered: "I found carob trees in the world when I was born.
Just as my ancestors planted for me so I, too, plant for my children."

— *Ta'anit* 23a

## Guardners

The Lord God
took the man
and placed him in
the Garden of Eden,
to cultivate
and to guard it.
— *Genesis 2:15*

## Jasmine and Rose

*(for Lebanon and Meteora)*
Upon entering the garden
I recognized your cryptic face
in an orchard
of fragrant flowering trees

We wandered
the valley of
monks and mystics
taking refuge in
an astonishingly
empty cave
soul-soaked
in jasmine
and rose

## ON GENIUS

*Everyone is a genius. But if you judge a fish by its ability to climb a tree, it will live its whole life believing that it is stupid.*
— Albert Einstein

We often arrogate the term "genius" to the exclusive realm of the intellect, but it could just as legitimately refer to physical, emotional or spiritual attributes. Thematic phenomena as diverse as time and place have a genius (*genius loci*), as do nations and biological species.

The word genius was traditionally used to describe an *external* tutelary deity, spirit or guardian of a person or place. It was appreciated as a guiding spirit that attended a person throughout their life. The common modern usage, however, has *internalized* the term. Genius has now been transformed into an expression that describes an individual's most outstanding qualities or exceptional talents in any number of realms. Some examples include being very smart or a savant (intellectual genius); handsome, beautiful, athletic or strong (physical genius); empathetic and benevolent (emotional genius); or mystical (spiritual genius).

According to these various usages, it could be argued that everyone—even everything—possesses a guiding spirit. What we do with it is quite another thing. Human consciousness has the power to cultivate, stimulate and amplify its native-born genius into expressions of exceptional output. Or, as is often the case, not to develop its full potential and let it go to waste. Not every seed germinates; not every genius flowers.

## ON HAPPINESS

Happiness makes me sad. I'm not referring to genuine happiness, but rather to the phenomenon of commercial happiness that is marketed from every conceivable media niche.

Happiness is big business, retail therapy, a temporary fix, an emotional drug. "You want to be happy?" they ask. "Then buy this car, wear those clothes, go on vacation, give to my charity, save our planet, lose that weight."

Happiness has become a burden, a dizzying series of magical resolutions and commercial panaceas. Stress and depression lurk in its shadow.

What is happiness anyway? In our rather young secular culture, we have abandoned much of the traditional wisdom of the past but have not yet developed the stories that give meaning to our lives. It takes time to mature; it is a generational process of shared experiences that must patiently ferment. Most of us are satisfied with a conditional happiness that is dependent on small victories and fortuitous coincidences. But there must be a deeper sense of happiness.

Does happiness come with meaning, with a coherent explanation for everything? Is it something to be achieved, or felt, or is it a state of being? There are many types of happiness. There is temporary happiness like that felt upon the first blush of love, completing a challenge or winning a prize; a medium contentment that reflects a general satisfaction with life; and then there is an ecstatic sense of enlightenment based upon transcendent metaphysics. Adherents of various world religions can mean vastly different things when speaking about how to attain happiness. The path to salvation for one leads to hell for another.

I wonder why the human psyche is so addicted to happiness? What evolutionary function does it perform? When we are feeling down we look to artificial stimulants, hedonistic pleasures and other psychological addictions to relieve distress and cheer ourselves up. We self-medicate. That generally seems to be tolerable behaviour, a reprieve from the necessary laws that bind society, but the repercussions are often filled with regret.

Until that day when world peace permeates the planet, I can be happy but only for a moment; I can laugh but not fully. My joy is anchored in your suffering. Until we can be happy together I would rather mourn with you than be happy by myself.

*This piece was first published in the Vancouver Sun in 2012 for a series conceived by Douglas Todd. – Ed.*

## ON HOLOCAUST

Everyday Madness
led to the Holocaust,
the eruption fueled
by the accumulated frustrations,
the constant discontents
with our daily lives.

The burden of consciousness
overwhelms us so we,
as a percentage of our species,
choose the dictator,
the conspiracy,
the fractured narrative
we insist will solve our problems.

The victims were double damned:
Innocent blank slates
upon which perpetrators
projected their darkening shadows
and sanctified their distorted beliefs.
Even, or especially, the Nazis,
the Saints of Sin,
justified murder
as they busied themselves
with cleansing the world.
They killed babies
but saved bullets
by grabbing tiny ankles
and smashing wailing heads
against random stoic trees and
farmers' stone-studded walls.
They thus fulfilled their Oaths,
performed their duty
with a sense of dedicated obedience
in the macabre step dance of war.

"Where is our reward?" they wondered
from the bunkers of defeat.
"How could the world not understand;
why don't they reward us
for our devoted work?
We have purified the world;
done you a great favour;
sacrificed for history
under the enlightened guidance
of der Führer and our superior
Doctors of Doom."

*Madness*, of course.
Until victims are piled beyond
what used to be called Heaven,
and Hell itself posts a No Vacancy sign
in neon
flashing red
reflected on tear-soaked parking lots,
the kind I see through the third floor
back-stained window
of my secret seedy hotel.
The entire world lives there
in a state of violated dignity,
marching two by two
as sorry captive creatures
towards the landlord Herr Hitler's
floundering dystopian ark.

And so it goes
in every generation,
until a greater justice calls forth
from the blood-beaten earth
and a truce between the Powers,
exhausted from battle,
disfigured by dispute,
is reluctantly concluded.

But only until next time arrives,
as it always does,
in the grip of cyclical insanity
when the rhythm of war
bursts from the human beast
once again,
camouflaged beneath

a finely tailored suit
of reasoned justifications
as if trying to create a second wave
of illusion's first impressions.
Never Again! we promise,
Never Again! we vow
over the bodies of our crucified gods.
And then, as addicts drawn
to their drug of choice,
humanity repeats its manic chorus.
It's what we do best.
Forgive us. . . .

## ON IMPERFECTION

What a relief to be imperfect! And yet I still habitually fall back into old, judgmental ways. Pursuit of the Ideal is built into the human mind, an apparently useful phenomenon that has claimed its position upon our psychic shelves. It has resulted in many noble but tattered thoughts, irrigated with the tears of wounded wisdom.

I remind myself to occasionally surrender to the humble and celebrate the stale. To welcome imperfection as it is, embrace that which is ordinary and accept the still incomplete. To honour peeling paint, the rough of rust and crown of well-earned patina. I am more comfortable with subtle shadows than overly manicured technologies.

What a relief to dedicate time for a midweek sabbath and a walk in nature's uncultivated garden where leaves fall where they may, blossoms bloom in annual renewal and fruit ripens in fulfillment of its unspoken destiny. Where weeds and summer-coloured wild flowers decorate the dust and century-old trees that once seemed immortal now dry with age and return to this good earth.

## ON KNOWLEDGE

*It's not the darkness we fear, it's the light behind the door.*
*It's not the answer we can't hear, it's the question we won't ask.*
— *Communion* by Daniel MacIvor

How often do we deny unexpected opportunities that come our way and resist related tests that are imposed upon us? How often do we limit our vision and actually fear the success about which we dream? At times it feels as if leaving our familiar selves and stepping into a greater persona could be a risk. The immensity of it all—including the associated responsibilities—may intimidate us as we wrestle with a complex world of vast challenges and startling wonders. It is important, however, to remember that the Unknown Infinite is not just large, distant and impersonal; it is also intimate, immediate and caring.[28]

In the passionate pursuit of the Universal Essence and in the name of an authentic encounter with Reality, I have embraced dedicated guidance from experienced elders while learning to accept measured boundaries and necessary discipline.

In the midst of this tenacious journey, I have welcomed sleepless nights exploring knowledge and travelled the world in search of wisdom. I have suffered humiliation and confusion but have also trembled with joy and been blessed with gratitude. I have forged myself into an empty vessel prepared to receive the collected discoveries of the generations and, in return, I endeavour to contribute that which emerges from the wellspring of my agitated and yet galvanized soul. We must make fear our friend and shadows our companions: they, too, are agents of astonishing growth.

## ON LIBRARIES

*Make books your friends*

Books, and all they represent, are our friends. Some of us are also friends of the book. Those who support libraries do so in keeping with the advice of the 12th century French-Jewish philosopher, Yehudah ibn Tibbon, who advised his son—*Oseh sefa're'ha haver'ha.*

> Make your books your companions. Let your cases and shelves be your orchards and gardens. Bask in their beauty [as if in paradise]. Harvest their fruit, gather their roses, collect their spices and myrrh. When your soul becomes weary [of one volume], move from garden to garden, from furrow to furrow and from one perspective to a new panorama. Then your desire will be refreshed and your soul filled with delight.

> Libraries, museums and archives are temples for recording information and understanding knowledge. In this quickly moving world, many of us have lost a sense of context, of where we came from and the wisdom of tradition. Among the reasons that libraries continue to be one of the most visited sites in all parts of the world is that they provide deep roots nurtured by the past and unfurled wings projecting us into the future. The public library, including its online incarnations, is the People's House of Lifelong Learning. Literacy —whether garbed in letters or the waving wind (for nature also speaks the seventy languages of all that exists)—is a vehicle to one's destination. Indeed, it may be the destination itself.

## ON MUSEUMS

Museums are inspired creatures. They are cajoled into existence by the lithe spirit of memory and are often temples—some grand, others humble—to the Muse of History, an unforgiving master that hides none yet protects all. Museums offer deep reflections in timeless mirrors for as long as we can, or dare, see.

Are we, ourselves, not also living museums? Do we not carry within us the memories of forever and the reach for exceedingly impossible goals? Are our faces not etched with the story of our lives, and do our eyes not betray both the spark and the tears of all our eternities?

Our bodies are maps for the literate, for those who would read us; our minds, treasures for those who would search us; our feelings, songs for those who would sing us; and our spirits still soar beyond the painful abuse of this world's temporary pilgrimage.

Surely, our journeys are permeated with a soulful metamorphosis—layered, profound and breathless—so much so that, in the end, we finally come to appreciate that we are all museums.[29]

## ON NAZIS

The Nazis didn't just kill people, they murdered love, hope and the last vestiges of decency.

They perfected murder; shamed humanity. That, after all the commentary, is their only legacy.

Words fail me yet silence, after a moment or a lifetime, cannot be our final response.

## ON PEACE

The entire planet is the proverbial Ark floating in the cosmic waters of creation. We are all passengers on Noah's global boat; Buckminster Fuller referred to our world as Spaceship Earth.

The question is: will we persist in being a Ship of Fools or will we learn to promote dialogue, peaceful coexistence and mutual understanding among people of all cultures?

Being suspicious of the *other* is natural. It is a defense mechanism, a reaction that affords protection. It is a ubiquitous operative principle whether in biology or politics. We could not survive without it; our immune system relies on it for health. But the *other* can also be complimentary, as in aesthetics. It is the basis of sexual attraction and the preservation of the species.

In this bivalent world, we must let the Rose be our teacher and the Bee serve as our guide. The flower has beauty and fragrance but also comes armed with thorns; the pollinator produces honey but not without the threat of a sting.

Knowing when to be wary and when to embrace the other is a basis of cooperative peace. It is possible to sit and sing together, to eat and speak as one, but in the process we need to remember not to abandon justice, for it will provide structure for our love and a vessel for our tenderness.

Some of our religious and political leaders have highjacked Heaven and subjugated the Earth. They purport to tell us what God thinks, what he does, what she wants.

Meanwhile, there are many ways to honour our traditions and show reverence to our beliefs:

> If you want to worship, care for the stranger.
> If you want to pray, then play with the children.

If you want to sacrifice, feed the hungry.

If it's prophecy you desire, then go out and make the future.

It it's knowledge you crave, then search for it as treasure, build schools to educate others so that eventually each one can teach one, and so that "the Earth will be filled with knowledge as the waters cover the sea."[30]

Our challenge is to be as active in pursuing peace as we are in waging war. There is no automatic result or pre-ordained conclusion. It is up to each one of us, fierce yet peaceful warriors.

*Excerpts from Keynote Speech on "Peaceful Coexistence" at the First Annual Dialogue and Friendship Dinner for the Intercultural Dialogue Institute, May 24, 2016, Roundhouse Community Centre, Exhibition Hall, Vancouver. — Ed.*

## ON PILGRIMAGE

*It is not down in any map; true places never are.*
— Herman Melville, *Moby Dick*.

Our entire lives are a pilgrimage, a personal journey through the unfolding of a greater continuum. Whether here at home or on distant roads to seemingly impossible locations (there are even certain destinations that you can't get to by going anywhere), pilgrimage remains a significant means towards understanding existence.

Pilgrimage presents both a challenge and an opportunity: those who are conscious of the meaning of their travels have a greater chance of achieving their goals. And yet one must also make room for getting lost and setting aside time for serendipitous assignations with unexpected phenomena. What may at first seem like an inconvenient detour often ends up defining the journey. If it is only the rational mind that controls the itinerary then the physical traveller may achieve her goal but the wandering soul will have been denied a greater adventure.

Those goals may be all-encompassing knowledge or self-determination; they may involve the community at large or prove to be a singular search for the object of one's desire. Pilgrimage embraces physical, spiritual, emotional and intellectual efforts. Accomplishments are achieved in the heart as much as the mind and in time as much as space. Some pilgrims travel to give thanks, others to seek forgiveness or to ask for healing, love or power. Some wander in search of the Other; many to know the Self. All must travel very far to know that which was always near.[31]

## ON POETRY

Poetry is a mystic art. It intuits expression and gives voice to the transcendent. Poetry translates ineffable essence into ten thousand languages of heaven on earth. It is the utterance of mysteries in the guise of the all-too-familiar.

Poetry is a noble art that inspires those who encounter it to achieve greater lives, to rededicate themselves to astonishing ideals of a better world. Yet it is also a base art, injured and numb, unbearably burdened, infinitely textured, humbled and filled with tears.

Poetry is the budding of blooms and the fading of petals; it is water and wind and the still turning point at the heart of it all. It is passioned seduction, servant of secrets and scent of forever in kaleidoscopic gardens fertilized by ever-becoming dreams.

The poet is a living manifestation of beauty, rhythm, struggles and sound. The poet is more than a rhyming couplet; s/he is also a sensitive barometer of society's moods. Poetry is a key when all doors are locked. Even though the laureate may carry the code, it will still be up to us to embrace the barrier and appear on the other side.

*YW wrote these lines to Vancouver City Councillor Elizabeth Ball when she introduced a motion to establish a Poet Laureate on October 17, 2006. It was passed unanimously and Wosk subsequently established an endowment to support "the people's poet." — Ed.*

## ON PRESENTATIONS

Whenever you make a speech, you are really involved in five.

The first is the one you think of making.
The second is the one you prepare.
The third is the one you actually deliver.
The fourth is the one the audience hears.
And the fifth is the one that, upon returning home,
you realize what you should have said.

*Y.W. heard this wisdom when he was twelve years old. He didn't understand it at the time but never forgot it. He says it applies to any presentation through which we attempt to communicate. —Ed.*

## ON PSYCHE

The root meaning of the Greek work *psyche* is "breath, life, spirit or soul." It was also the word for butterfly, a metaphor for the one who undergoes complete metamorphosis in the process of achieving one's potential.

In Greek mythology, Psyche was the personification of the soul. She took the form of the most beautiful woman, one who attracted the attention of Eros (Cupid in the Roman version), the God of Romantic

Love and Desire. After many challenges, they eventually succeeded in sharing a passionate love. Psyche was made immortal so that the two paramours—the embodiment of soulful love—could spend eternity together.

The word therapy derives from the Latin and Greek *therapia*. Its literal meaning is "curing or healing." Just as we have doctors for our bodies, so we have guides to assist with emotional turmoil and imbalances in our brains. Medicine men and shamans, ordained ministers and priests used to fill this role. Today, the secular soul catchers are therapists, counsellors and psychiatrists, social workers or trusted friends.

Even a glimpse of an ephemeral butterfly in the fullness of a verdant garden still has the power to heal. It is the embrace of Psyche and Eros, the ideal towards which we are eternally drawn.

## ON PSYCHOGEOGRAPHY

*We do not come into this world; we come out of it,*
*as leaves from a tree.*
*As the ocean waves, the universe peoples.*
— Alan Watts

Psychogeography is the psyche, or soul, of the earth. It describes how the planet affects us and how we influence the planet, how the Earth possesses not just a body but also a global brain, and how all that emerged from this celestial orb is related in a vast interactive ecology.

By generating the term psychogeography, I am giving myself permission to put our species into perspective, not just theoretically but viscerally. Instead of placing people at the centre or elevating them to the apex of creation (anthropomorphism), I am trying to experience a kinship with all that ever existed, from heavenly hosts to those injured by cruel circumstances and from interstellar dust that once burned bright-forever to the embers of extinguished ashes. I also strive to connect with the stillborn and with all possible permutations that have remained mired in potential but will never see the light of day.

Psychogeography is a marriage of mind and matter, the correspondence between psyche and soma, a principle that extends throughout all that exists. It is a private art more than a public science. It is an intoxicating potion of the rare, the commonplace and the exotic; a conversation between talking trees, listening landscape, weaving spiders and receptive firmament; it is stillness and constancy blended with an ever-active state of becoming.

Psychogeography is returning to the original meaning of "geography," i.e. *geo graphia*, "earth writing," the earth authoring its own narrative and we becoming literate enough, once again, to read it. It is the cosmos becoming conscious of itself through the agency of human awareness. As a practice, it is deeply humbling and only shared now in the hushed tones of an awkward observation here in the novelty section of the *New Life Joke Shop*.

## ON QUEST

Our quests have been long and arduous. Over the years, after too many opportunities that ended in regret, we, along with Kierkegaard, learned to dare greatly:

> "Have I dared wrongly?
> Oh well, then life will help me with the punishment.
> But if I have not dared at all, who will help me then?"

Although we may have worked hard and studied until time abandoned its clock, although we chased sleep from our eyes and rest from our exhausted bodies, dreamt with the stars and travelled to the very ends of the earth in search of wisdom, we may still feel empty, aware that there is so much more to learn, to know, to be, to do.

What *was* achieved is only a small percentage of what *could have* been implemented. Regarding this, King Solomon affirmed that "No one dies with even half their desires fulfilled."[32]

## ON STORY

The universe began with story, is sustained through story and it will end with story. It began with story composed of individual letters, each one weighed and measured, then strung together in the weaving of words. The Holy One began to tell such stories in the silence of unformed space, in the stillness of time not yet born. There was no ear to hear nor was there a mind to comprehend that two thousand years before the heavens and the earth, seven things were created. Among them was the primordial Torah written with black fire upon white fire.

The darkened letters contained that which was revealed—the spoken word—while the white-fired celestial parchment, containing unutterable secrets, supported them. White Fire was the realm where words had no influence, where pregnant silence and intuitive knowing dwell as one.

But soon, from out of an astonishingly empty presence, the Creator spoke its story and the world tumbled into being: "Let there be light, and there was light. Let there be a heaven and an earth, oceans and life. And it was so."

Stories create worlds; they also destroy them. Just read the headlines and ask your dreams.

## ON TECHNOLOGY

We often feel like citizen-soldiers. The front lines begin at our fingertips, our bodies have become imaginal battlefields, our eyes are seared with atrocities, our ears deafened by violent explosions and torn by piteous weeping of those caught in the crossfire. We are being virtually attacked every day. Trauma, fatigue, depression and anxiety are the burdens we bear, all sponsored by global communications technologies that seek to monetize conflict while championing particular opinions.

We may isolate in relative safety behind locked doors and fortified homes, and yet the world persists on invading through wireless electronic devices that have extended our senses and stretched our consciousness. We are under attack in the comfort of our living rooms, assaulted on multiple fronts by climate change and the desperate parade of surging immigrants, the threat of nuclear radiation, polluted oceans and burning forests, economic inflation, too much crime and not enough housing, as well as daily war images of falling rockets and disfigured bodies. The private has become public while the public is now global.

Technology has also allowed us to know the opposition, the other, more intimately. We can access the enemy mind, scheme with populist presidents, be radicalized by zealots, and strategize with autocratic generals or fanatical regimes at the touch of a button. Many of us are overwhelmed by the incessant technological soap opera, the algorithms that manipulate us and the artificial intelligence that blurs the lines between realities.

There is, however, still a third option. It is a kind of stoic sabbatical that permits us to be aloof and distant, objective and unattached to outcomes. It is an attitude in which we allow ourselves to observe this entire drama unfold both as a tragedy and as a comedy, sympathetic for one team or the other but attached to none. We have, for the most part, lost a sense of certainty.

Perhaps, as humanity evolves (or devolves?) to the next level of awareness, that is not all a negative outcome. We are immersed in a liminal state of perception, one that finds us, at least temporarily, in a constant state of confusion. As a reaction, the mind is sometimes drawn to take a break from the ubiquitous Game and, like an objective philosopher or an innocent newborn, we retreat into becoming passive observers, indifferent to the outcome in the midst of global Lilliputian disputes.

Indifference, however, must never be a conclusion but only a momentary withdrawal, an understandable reaction to the flood of challenges. Stepping back in order to gain perspective will then encourage us to step back up with a more measured and judicious use of our technologies including the basic inborn ones such as our five senses. Such is the greater lesson from nature's cyclical rhythm where the sun sets every night giving us an opportunity to recover from yesterday's actions and to dream of a better tomorrow.

## ON WAR

And so it *was* known;
knowledge did seep out,
but the burden of such knowledge
was too inconvenient
resulting in perpetrators being protected
by our sheer disbelief
or our fear of consequences
for knowing too much.

We preferred another naïve day
in the theme park of our
expertly procrastinating minds
instead of having to disturb routine,
or lay down our lives
for the sake of others' bad behaviour.

Who could blame those who knew
but did not act
or those who were too busy living
to sacrifice themselves for someone else's war?

Such is the latent psychosis
that defines human consciousness:
We are both angel and devil,
lover and tortured death incarnate.

## ON WORK

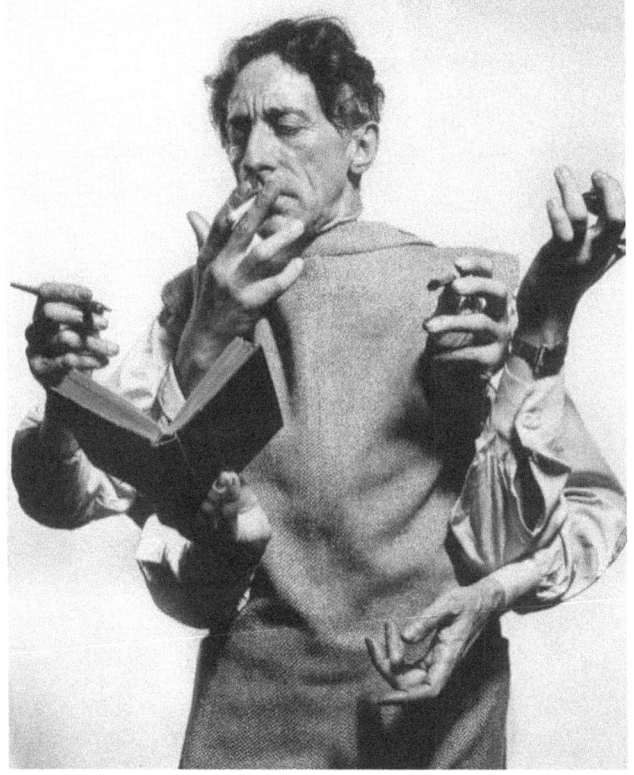

"*You are not expected to complete the work, but neither are you free to evade it.*"
— Rabbi Tarfon[33]

The full quotation is: "Rabbi Tarfon said: The day is short and there is much work; the labourers are lazy but the wage is great and the Master of the House is insistent. He also used to say: You are not expected to complete the work, but neither are you free to evade it."

Comparable aphorisms are found in other cultures, including that by Hippocrates (c. 460–c. 370 BCE), the Greek "Father of Medicine," who reflected in his introduction to a medical text about the relative shortness of life compared to the length of time it takes to master the techniques of healing. His words were translated into Latin as *Vita brevis, ars longa,* that in turn are rendered into English as "Life is short and art is long" (the word *art* representing the "art of the craft or technical virtuosity of the discipline"). Geoffrey Chaucer, the "Father of English Literature," writing in the fourteenth century, penned a similar sentiment—"The lyf so short, the craft so long to lerne"—as the first line of *The Parlement of Foules* (The Parliament of Birds).

Although our minds may imagine omniscience—having infinite awareness, understanding and insight—our intellect struggles to achieve that state of knowing, and our bodies lag even farther behind. No matter how heroic our efforts, we are ultimately limited by the impossible task of learning, doing and becoming everything. Technologies have extended our reach but we still have a long way to go.

Humbled, we must finally accept that some projects are communal tasks stretching from past through future generations. Even though we may only represent a singular cell in the body of our temporary species, we are still encouraged not to despair but to fulfill our individual lives. This is what Rabbi Tarfon meant.

# THE FUTURE OF KNOWLEDGE:
## CONTEMPLATING MUSEUMS

*The universe is a museum without walls*

Technology extends from the use of primitive tools to an appreciation for how the cosmos expresses itself. We are all technologies. This essay considers the relationship between museums, individuals and technologies as we enter a brave but often confusing new world.

### *Information, knowledge, wisdom and imagination*
The search to discover the meaning of reality has a long history. Such explorations have been around since *In the Beginning* and will continue to inhabit the world until the end of time. What are the distinctions between information, knowledge and wisdom, three very different words that are often mistakenly used as synonyms?

*Information* can be mined anywhere between the poles of a singular bit of datum to a massive collection of circumstances. It is an undifferentiated collection of individual facts and even fictions.

*Knowledge* is the organization of disjointed information into coherent systems.[34]

*Wisdom*, however, requires fermentation.[35] It only comes with age and experience. It is atavistic, reflective and partakes of dreamtime.[36]

Rainer Maria Rilke expressed this patient maturing into wisdom in his poignant passage *For the Sake of a Single Verse:*[37]

> It is not yet enough to have memories. One must be able to forget them when they are many and have the great patience to wait until they return. For the memories themselves are not important. Not until they have changed into blood within us, to glance and gesture, nameless and no longer to be distinguished from ourselves—only then can it happen that in a most rare hour the first word of a verse arises in their midst and goes forth from them.

That is deep wisdom. Those words took courage to write and composure to live. That is what Aldus Manutius, the Venetian Renaissance scholar printer, integrated into his *impresa* depicting a dolphin wrapped around an anchor accompanied by the Latin words *Festina Lente*— "Make haste, slowly."

When considering these various categories of perception, however, it is also important not to abandon fantasy and imagination. It is instructive to consider Einstein's observation: "When I examined myself and my methods of thought, I came to the conclusion that the gift of fantasy has meant more to me than my talent for absorbing positive knowledge." This has also been expressed as: "Imagination is more important than knowledge."

While respecting tradition along with the venerable wisdom that it offers, one also has the authority to be creative iconoclasts. Museums, which themselves are technologies, are organized according to several working models none of which are intrinsically good or bad. We are not transgressing some cosmic law when we redesign in whole or in part. There is no one answer. The following quote from

Stephen Weil, a seminal thinker in the field of arts and museums, exemplifies this point:

> Museums are our own human creation—neither based on any changeless ideal nor occurring as a fact of nature—and they are a creation that we are free to shape and reshape as may best suit our needs.[38]

## *Technology*

I am using the word "technology" in its widest possible connotation, not just to apply to machinery, electronics and automation but rather to encompass all the arts and building blocks of civilization from physical mechanics to grammar and fine arts.

Marshall McLuhan spoke about technologies as extensions of our bodies and amplifications of our minds. Shoes, for example, are extensions of our feet; clothes a replication of skin; binoculars and microscopes augment our eyes; weapons extend our arms; specialized tools replicate hands; telephones echo our ears; computers multiply our minds; and so on. Over time we domesticated animals, invented the wheel, built wagons and boats, then, in more recent centuries, we developed the train, automobile and airplane, until now we are "knock, knock, knockin' on heaven's door"[39] with interplanetary space travel and orbiting telescopes that are attempting to peer back in time to the inception of the known universe.[40]

In Lewis Mumford's groundbreaking 1967 book, *The Myth of the Machine: Technics & Human Development*, he observed that "[Humanity's] great discoveries were not physical tools nor the technics based on them. A stone axe endures and can be examined by an archaeologist; it is natural that he should lay stress on it. Vastly more important to early [humanity], however, were the intangible things that have left little or no trace—ritual, social organisation, and, above all, the tremendous invention of language."[41]

It could be argued that today we only use "tech" to refer to applied science but the word science itself can be traced to the Greek root *scientia* meaning knowledge, i.e. any knowledge, not just that with technological implications.

The Roman philosopher Cicero praised the human ability to transform the environment and create a "second nature." Biblical literature also described people as being created *b'tselem Elokim,* in the reflected image of God.[42] We became the Great Imitators of deities, *imitatio Dei,* even as we strove for originality. All that humans do is involved in discovering nature and then imitating, amplifying or recombining it.[43]

A further dimension to the meaning of technology is that it is not just an anthropocentric construct but rather a cosmological constant. It exists everywhere at all times. Just as nature is a universal technology so we, too, are nature's technologies that continue to evolve towards an as yet unknown purpose. We may have free will up to a point but we are also unconscious servants to the Essence of Existence that expresses itself through us.

Although we cannot yet say with certainty that we know why the cosmos exists, there are many theories. Douglas Adams, author of *A Hitchhiker's Guide to the Galaxy,*[44] humorously conjectured that "There is a theory which states that if ever anyone discovers exactly what the Universe is for and why it is here, it will instantly disappear and be replaced by something even more bizarre and inexplicable. There is another theory which states that this has already happened."[45]

Some theological and philosophical schools of thought speculate that matter, time and space always existed and always will. Certain scientific models concur.

Other mystical doctrines describe a sequence of emanations originating from an Infinite non-corporeal Entity that—in a series of ongoing acts of creation—cascade through a number of metaphorical step-down transformers.[46] *Creatio ex nihilo*; something from nothing.

A beginning implies an end with a temporary existence between. Consequently, Jean Houston described us as "people of the parenthesis," those who inhabit the Great In-between.

Just as humans use technologies such as tools and speech, so the universe uses earth, air, fire and water, gravity, electromagnetism and stellar thermonuclear fusion. The underlying principle remains the same, extending from the microcosmic to the macrocosmic, from the single atom to the size of all reality. *All that exists, including us, are technologies.*

The universe itself is the Master Museum, containing every wondrous artefact and mundane matter, making no distinction in the Grand Crucible of Creation. Whereas we once arrogated technology as a distinctly human endeavour, it can now be appreciated as a commonly shared adventure. We are merely local ambassadors of a universal consciousness that curates the cosmos.

I am not in any way denigrating the human species, although there is much to criticize.

We are not just an encapsulated bundle of flesh and bones but rather a grand experiment, a partnership of matter and mind. The technologies that combine to make us human are not necessarily all tangible, obvious or perceptible to the limitations of our five common senses. Buckminster Fuller, the great inventor, architect and global systems visionary, recognized that "99% of who you are is invisible and untouchable." There is also the more-subtle sixth sense, in addition to the hundreds of even more ethereal faculties that populate the mindscape of our unfolding consciousness.

Our minds, we ourselves, may be utilitarian technologies but we are also impregnated with magic. The poet, author and naturalist Diane Ackerman recognized this when she wrote: "If a mind is just a few pounds of blood, dream, and electric, how does it manage to contemplate itself, worry about its soul, do time-and-motion studies, admire the shy hooves of a goat, know that I will die, enjoy all the grand and lesser mayhems of the heart?"[47]

### Innovation

If technology is the thing, innovation [derived from *novus,* or new] is the fuel. Technology is object, item, matter and material. Innovation partakes of subject, ideal, movement, mutation and modification.

We are both fascinated with, and intimidated by, innovation, by what the unknown future may bring. As *The Amazing Criswell: Plan 9 From Outer Space* once remarked: "We are all interested in the future because that is where you and I will spend the rest of our lives."[48]

*What is innovation and why are we enamoured by it?* What is its seductive, even erotic, power? Continuing innovation presents unlimited possibilities, opportunities and improvement. We use stirring words to describe that which is emerging, terms like front line, avant-garde, newest technology, leading edge, vanguard, new wave, revolutionary and pioneering. Innovation represents birth, dynamic success and renewal. It is also used to sell products. Even if we already have them we can now buy "the new and improved" spin-offs that entice with smaller or larger, faster or more powerful added features that are often beyond our personal or institutional needs.

Not only are we assaulted by efforts to monetize innovative technologies but we also challenge ourselves to be *au courant* with statements like this one attributed to Gelett Burgess: "If in the last few years you haven't discarded a major opinion or acquired a new one, check your pulse. You may be dead."

Innovation is imagined as the reincarnated self, the messianic vision fulfilled and a taste of the World to Come. It is the promise of new beginnings, continuation of the species and of potential achievement just when we might be feeling wounded by decades of wrestling with life's hidden gravities. The spirit of innovation fuels a constantly agitated birthing into a simultaneous profusion of emerging dimensions. Every moment serves as witness to a revelation of time into space and a resurrection of genesis from the detritus of discarded matter.[49]

When we discuss Innovation in its widest sense we must also ask where it came from and where it is going? Why creation, death and renewal? Does Innovation as an animating force of Universal Consciousness have a purpose, a goal towards which it is moving or is it simply a self-sustaining phenomenon? The power of creation does not just belong to the past, a prisoner of a distant propagation. It is a constantly reoccurring act of renewal. The urge to innovate is the cause of our curiosity, our art and desires. It is why all creatures procreate just as the planets are attracted to the sun, a cosmic love story of celestial proportions.

I think of Innovation as *Eros*. The Greek Eros was a primordial god, son of Chaos, but later tradition made him the mischievous son of Aphrodite, goddess of sexual love, beauty and fertility. In psychology and philosophy, Eros has been used as a principle of Life Energy as exemplified by passionate love and physical desire. Its opposite is *Thanatos,* that which leads towards death, destruction, and the return of both physical and metaphysical matter to nothingness.

Innovation is the fuel that drives technology. Innovation is the spirit; technology the body. Technology is noun; Innovation verb.

### *Too much or not enough innovative technology?*

There is a danger that museums—along with universities, libraries and related institutions—may rely too heavily upon innovative technology to solve their problems. Some pundits disparage society and its institutions for what has been termed "an infatuation with technology." It is not always a case of "Build it and they will come." We sometimes invest in excessive upgrades and end up taking costly write-offs or even having to close the doors altogether.

On the other hand many institutions *are* underwhelming in their presentations and stifling in their bureaucratic attitudes. They exemplify the use of the label "museum" to mean "a boring collection of dusty keepsakes." They have been tagged with derogatory descriptives criticizing them as musty administrative crypts, graveyards for stuff, tombs for inanimate things that have been collected-and-caged, smug and lacking in vitality or relevance. Instead of being the Wizards of Worlds we end up constructing a Temple of Doom, one that the visitor perceives as a negative and inhibiting experience. We become the threatening voices reprimanding visitors not to take photos, not to express themselves above a whisper, not to sing, dance, eat or be nourished in the presence of the exhibits.[50]

We may work for months, sometimes years, developing strategic plans that include general improvements and vast amounts of updated technologies. Some end up investing too much in these new technologies and others not enough. Instead of complementing our exhibits, misused technologies end up obfuscating the visitor experience. They become a barrier not a mirror and are worn as masks, isolating the personal, human engagement behind a protective face of neutral mechanics.

And yet new technologies are important to the life of museums and attractive to our patrons.[51] At times, it turns out that we just haven't thought the whole thing through well enough. Dr. Bette Stephenson, a former Conservative minister of colleges and universities in Ontario, was quoted as saying "Universities are trying to meet 21st-century problems with 16th-century philosophy, and working in an 18th-century organization…. If they could just get their centuries together, they might solve their problems."[52] With some emendations, the same might be said for museums.

### *A river without banks in a world without borders*

We are a pivotal generation experiencing the greatest revolution in technology since Gutenberg invented moveable type in the 15th century. The print revolution resulted in an enormous democratization of knowledge with information flowing more freely than ever before. The digital revolution has multiplied that effect many times over.

An algorithmic flow of instantaneous communications has been released—a river without banks in a world without borders. We have now harnessed our combined brainpower and live in a synergistic Global Brain.[53]

This massive burst of technological innovation has not come without a price. Every area of our lives—indeed of the entire planet—has been affected. As we learn to adapt to a new mindscape some among us suffer from loss of meaning. Conflicts extend from internal struggles to world wars as headlines warn about Climate Change inflamed by environmental degradation. Doomsday Clocks continue to tick into a future that is collapsing upon itself. Whereas we once invented technologies, technologies are now manipulating us. As new benchmarks for accessing information arise we are undergoing a reconfiguring of our biological neural networks to include a greatly expanded sense of both outer and inner space.

It has not always been a seamless process of adaptation. Anxiety and depression are at all-time highs. Many have lost their bearings, their centre, their direction.[54] What once was certain and stable has now been replaced by a New Story,[55] by the next Theory of Relativity. We are being asked to evolve at an unprecedented pace and as Woody Allen quipped: "More than any other time in history, mankind faces a crossroads. One path leads to despair and utter hopelessness. The other, to total extinction. Let us pray we have the wisdom to choose correctly."[56]

But all is not lost, for we are a resilient species. We may be a disoriented generation but let us also embrace that wonderful confusion. Walt Whitman once celebrated his many facets with this memorable declaration: "Do I contradict myself? Very well then I contradict myself, (I am large, I contain multitudes)."[57]

### *Inside Out: Telepresence in a digital age*
It used to be that if we wanted something we had to go somewhere

to get there, to be there. We had to physically trek to the museum, to the library, to the market. The Internet and other electronic media, however, have usurped some of the museum's purpose, domain, privilege and exclusivity.[58]

In an article published in the American Association of Museums' *Museum News,*[59] Mitchell and Strimpel observed that "In the past, being 'present' meant that your body was there. Now electronic tele-presence and asynchronous presence are additional possibilities. These are less intense than full face-to-face presence, but they can be achieved with greater convenience and at lower expenditure of time and resources. There is an emerging economy of presence."[60]

Museums, galleries and libraries used to be largely judged by the number of artefacts on display, holdings in storage or books on their shelves. The digital age has now blurred such definitions. In revamped libraries, books are just one source of information among many others and some librarians are referred to as Information Specialists, Information Architects, Knowledge Liaisons or Intelligence Managers.[61]

The many benefits, however, that accompany instantaneous access to an astounding amount of information and a worldwide network of museums signal a great transformation, one that had been ripening for thousands of years. We no longer have to go *out there,* for it is now *within us*; the external has been internalized. This may seem like somewhat of an exaggeration but it is evident by the technology that is in your pocket and purse—your smart phone and other personal communications devices.

Even they, however, are external accessories and therefore somewhat inconvenient. As technology gets ever-more sophisticated it will be more fully integrated into the human operating system. In the not-too-distant future innovative technologies will be surgically implanted within us. Virtual Reality and Artificial Intelligence will be complimented by *Brain-Technology Interfaces* that interact with the brain and neural structures to translate thought into action.[62]

Futurists envision "mind downloading" and "information uploading," a phenomenal feat especially considering that, theoretically speaking, there are 100 trillion synaptic connections in the brain, more neural connections, according to one estimate, than there are atoms in the universe.[63] Books, computers or other memory devices will no longer be necessary. Our thoughts will be directly transmitted and we will be able to access ubiquitous knowledge. The serpent in the garden—a symbol of the irrepressible power of rebellious Innovation—was correct about the transformative technology growing on the Tree at the Centre of the Garden: "When you partake of it your eyes will be opened and you shall be like God."[64]

Although we are among the most adaptable life forms on Earth and most of us eventually accommodate the parade of new technologies, others are wary of innovation and call it the devil's work. There have always been fearful reactions to new technologies. Train travel for example. Critics of early steam-spewing locomotives thought "that women's bodies were not designed to go at 50 miles an hour" and worried that "[female passengers'] uteruses would fly out of [their] bodies as they were accelerated to that speed." Others suspected that any human body might simply melt at high speeds.[65] Automobiles were called "devil wagons" and some Cassandras were concerned that speaking on the telephone would cause impropriety, possession or electrocution.

To further illustrate the nature of belonging to a metamorphic generation, of living inside out, listen to this ancient Hindu story:

> One day, while playing in the fields, little Krishna—who was an incarnation of the Hindu god Vishnu, something his mother, Yashoda, did not know at the time—secretly ate some mud. His friends went and told Yashoda about this. When Krishna returned home his mother scolded him. Krishna, like all children proclaiming their innocence,

replied that his friends were lying. His mother, knowing her son too well, told him: "If you have not taken any mud, then open your mouth. I shall see for myself." When Yashoda looked into his mouth, she was wonderstruck. She saw the entire cosmos: the mountains, the oceans, the planets, air, fire, moon and the stars in his small mouth."[66]

Even when Krishna is in the universe, the universe resides in Him.[67] This is the stage that humanity is approaching if we don't destroy one another and our precious planet first.

The speed of technological transformation is reminiscent of Alice in Wonderland who was told by the Queen of Hearts: "Now here, you see, it takes all the running you can do to keep in the same place. If you want to get somewhere else, you must run at least twice as fast as that."

### The next conversation

We are in the midst of the next Great Conversation. Ours is a swiftly evolving species but it started slowly. It used to take hundreds of thousands of years to graduate from one technology to another, then tens of thousands and soon only a few thousand years. That accelerated into a hundred years, then only a human generation or two. Today, technological generations are no longer measured in human terms but from the perspective of the products themselves. A new age of quantum computer technology is being born even as you read these words.[68]

It has been suggested that instead of reacting with anxiety, disdain or becoming Luddites, that we should replace fear of the unknown with curiosity. Remember that all these innovative technologies are part of human evolution, are extensions of our senses and are acts of Eros. As such, like love, we are attracted to them because they are either beautiful or useful.[69] Technologies are a natural manifestation of Universal Consciousness. They are not the enemy but rather a vehicle towards achieving our often unacknowledged desires and unknown destinations. Eros has taken us by the hand and never let us go.

### *Conclusion*

After reflecting upon the progression from random information to organized knowledge leading to mature wisdom, and after contemplating about an expanded appreciation of technology fuelled by innovation, I have arrived at some conclusions that may be applicable not only in cultural institutions but also for individuals.

Partner the old with the new just as dawn announces the liminal transition between night and day. Be on the cutting edge of new technologies but do not bankrupt yourself by becoming an overly-eager early adapter. By next year, the product will be twice as powerful and cost half as much.

Attitude, too, is an innovative and renewable technology, one that gleans generous returns. Give yourself permission to shine; to work harder and feel deeper; to radiate brilliance and genuine inspiration; to laugh with abandon and be moved to tears in the presence of beauty for that is true aesthetic alchemy. The future can be dire; at the same time it can be a stirring vision, one of innovative technology on a human scale, heart-centred and soul-sized.

Be an independent thinker; speak up and act out. Listen for the Muses themselves to guide you. These inner voices and eternal spirits are at your service.

You are also a Nation Builder. Sydney Jones, a past president of the Canadian Library Association, related the following anecdote that transpired when he was in a New York City cab and got into conversation with the driver. "This young man in his 20s had recently moved to the United States from India. After some time, he asked me and my colleagues what we did for a living. I responded that we were librarians. Without missing a beat, he replied, 'So you are nation-builders.' I looked at him, wondering what on earth he thought I had said. He saw my puzzled expression and added, 'You collect knowledge so that everyone may learn.'"[70]

Be bold; be brave. As someone fortunate to live during this pivotal era, it is not just your responsibility; it is also your birthright, your inheritance, your opportunity and your dream.

Don't be intimidated by the darkness for it, too, hovers over half the world and defines much of our inner lives. Look to the shadow as much as the light for they are twins in the duality of creation. In this regard, one of my favourite books is the intriguing *In Praise of Shadows* published in 1933 by the Japanese author Junichiro Tanizaki. It is an extended essay that contains "perfect descriptions of lacquerware under candlelight and women in the darkness of a house of pleasure. The result is a classic description of the collision between the shadows of traditional Japanese interiors and the dazzling light of the modern age."[71]

Technology is a synonym for all that exists. The future of technology is not a destination but rather a process of becoming. All existence is a choreographed dance, a *pas de deux* of dynamic and static forces. We, ourselves, are a sentient technology grounded in tradition, encouraged by innovation.

Each one of us is an entire world. Our bodies may be a temporary abode but our psyches fly on the wings of forever.

*A version of this essay was prepared as the closing Keynote Address for the British Columbia Museums Association Annual Conference in Kelowna, B.C., October 23, 2018. It is available as a podcast, "Universal Technologies and Innovations." Also see the online journal, The British Columbia Review, #479, "On the wings of forever," for another, more comprehensive, iteration. — Ed.*

The World Tree, whose roots descend deep into the underworld and branches stretch to the heavens, is depicted here as Yggdrasil in Norse mythology. Oroboros encircles the world; Yggdrasil upholds it. The World Tree nurtures all that is below and is, in turn, nourished by the heavens and the earth—a grand interweaving of all that exists.

# OROBOROS:[72]
# HOW THE WORLD
# CONSUMES & BIRTHS ITSELF

> *next spring*
> *I'll go out to the garden*
> *and with a stick*
> *plant myself*
> *and eat me in the fall*
> —Fred Wah[73]

The universe is a single cannibalistic organism, a self-sustaining unbroken circle; autonomous, terrifying and utterly unstoppable. Herbivore, carnivore, omnivore, orovore—the serpent devouring its own tail in an eternal vortex of renewal; its own creation and self-destruction; the endless knot, eternal return, historic recurrence.

Cosmological mechanics have evolved into an orchestra of energies in service to the One Meal. It is a circus inhabited by pollinators, predators and decomposers; swimmers, flyers, walkers and crawlers; by shape shifters, tricksters and masqueraders beneath a cloak of camouflage. Some, like leaves, effortlessly drop in self-sacrifice while others, such as prey, are reluctantly snatched so that the greater ecological maze might prevail. Consumables are part of an alchemical process, a parade of seasonal transformations no less than the transmutation of base metals into noble ones—lead into gold and corrupt characteristics into sublime soul. We witness nature's evolution from seed to fruit, roe to fish, calf to cow, and from egg to feathered fowl. Each one begets another until, at the expiry of their allotted time, they return to *Terra Mater* to fertilize ensuing generations.

Whether it be worm or whale, atom, Adam or astronomical phenomena, matter manifests as runway fashion—as models garbed in *haute couture* of iridescent feathers, burnished furs, warm wools and silken skins. One organism grows long necks to harvest high branches while another lumbers on tree-trunk legs; one flies on weightless wings or struts in peacock plumage while the multi-zoned oceans and seventy seas are astonished at their own aquatic affluence. There is evidence of hierarchy here, of one being hunted by another, serving as the unwilling offering in the daily menu of telluric fare.

### *Elixirs of milk and honey*

Food culture is a pilgrimage to discover the universal elixir. The Greeks spoke of *ambrosia* and the Hindus of *soma* or *amrita* that ensured anyone who ingested them their immortality. Milk is accorded related prestige. There are almost as many milk myths ministering to ancient cultures as there are stars that pave the Milky Way. The universe is draped in a shimmering gown of lactic lace from which creation emerged and continues to be sustained. Hoary streams of moon milk gush from nursing mothers, each one a goddess concealed beneath the masks of *maya*, survivor of love's last labour. Mother Moon bathed in blood of birth and overflowing as a fountain, spills her first ablution of breasted milk into the insistent mouths of ravenous newborns, forever to be fed.

The Philosopher's Stone morphs into Virgin's Milk, the tincture of transformation: Whoever drinks it is renewed; those who encounter it *in veritas* achieve immortality. Consider, also, semen, male milk poured as viscid broth flush with propagating seed in search of receptive ovum. And the milky sap of the Sacred Fig, the *Ficus religiosa* that sheltered the Buddha and encouraged his enlightenment. The fig leaf covered our first nakedness, a gift from the Omnipotent Creator turned modest tailor who taught us how to clothe embarrassment, assuage poverty and to give before being asked.

The Promised Land flows with fattened milk and immortal honey,[74] a virtuous substance that, like gold, does not spoil and whose sweetness bears learning upon the tongue. An aphrodisiac in metaphor and in deed, honey has powers of healing and skill in seduction. It is also associated with the sun for both are golden and givers of life. Mead, fermented honey, was drunk for a moon month —honeymoon—after marriage to ensure fertility. For the Celts it was the favoured drink of the immortal gods; the Norse identified it as the Mead of Inspiration and Poetry; and in Africa it was considered a sacred Liquid of Knowledge. These elixirs—*ambrosia, soma, amrita, lapis philosophorum,* milk and mead—are material equivalents of *Tat tvam asi,* Thou Art That of the Vedas. All things manifest from that imperceptible Essence.

### *House*

The house—whether in dream, allegory or actuality—corresponds to the body: Windows represent eyes, door is mouth, electricity is nervous system, plumbing digestive system and basement the unconscious. Each room, and how we perceive it, holds a message. The kitchen represents heart and hearth, nutrition and caregiving. It is scene of shared meals, social gatherings, intimate conversations, secret cabinets, well-worn memories, quiet reading, inherited recipes and the cutting/combining/cooking of ingredients to patiently nourish body and soul.

## *Table*

Tables can be austere—broken furniture veiled by tattered stained cloth—or king's royal cookery; any shape; private or public, invited or not; set according to function and seated according to protocol. Human consciousness turns us into meaning machines wherein a table used for ritual takes a simple meal and transforms it so that ceremonial meals attain cult status. Appreciated in such a light, the eating board becomes hierophant, a mediating altar between Heaven and Earth. As the venue of love incarnate, the table stands in the embrace of gravity attracted to all and all drawn to it. Upon this altar, a third of the world's population commemorates redemption of the First Food and celebration of the Last Supper. The Eucharist is the sacramental sharing of a common meal wherein one ingests the ritual wine-blood and body-bread. It also represents the union of male and female principles,[75] irrigated by the unifying cup, the shared chalice, the Holy Grail.

As an act of gratitude and in recognition of its ethereal provenance, there are those who bless every item on their plate before and then after eating. We greet holidays with incantations such as *ha lah ma'anyah*—"This is the bread of affliction that our ancestors ate in the land of Egypt. Let all who are hungry come and eat; let all who are in need come and partake." Foods become our teachers; they remind us that freedom is a daily struggle and that most of us—politically or psychologically—are still enslaved. Open now to welcome the afflicted. Quickly, before death do us part as always it will.

The planet itself is a true round table suspended in space, host to every meal, forum of feast and famine alike, caterer to the stars. It is the stage of diets, rituals, etiquette, festival fares and beggars' banquets. Even tragic starving victims—too weak to rise from grave-like ground as they feebly chew on old leather in a desperate attempt to extract another moment's sustenance—find timid place at her vacant lot.

## *Diet*

Diets are many; let me count the ways: Some eat when hungry, others when nervous; some suffer pathological eating disorders, others fast to enhance spiritual attributes. There are those who follow the Doctrine of Signatures, homeopathic and medical diets, personal, ideological, ethnic, religious or athletic diets. There are fussy eaters, gourmands and epicures, vegans, health food aficionados, as well as consumers of genetically modified Frankenfoods and junk foods laden with tens of artificial chemical ingredients, five kinds of sugar and petroleum-derived products.

Cuisine is enhanced with sensual stirrings: We are seduced by *sight*—colours, shapes, and plating presentations; *smell* of fragrant aromas; *feel* for firm and fresh, along with fingered tongue determining variegated textures; as well as the diverse indications of *taste*—sweet, sour, salty, bitter and umami. Taoists refer to varying degrees of the Life Force in everything. They know what edibles to choose and what to avoid, and strive to ultimately not even require victuals at all because one can theoretically be nurtured by absorbing cosmic *qi*, akin to Bergson's *élan vital*.

The Koran describes that which is *halal* (permissible) and *haram* (forbidden). The Bible introduces laws of hygiene and *kashrut*: Quadrupeds must have cloven hoofs and chew their cud; *kosher* fish also have two signs—fins and scales; permitted birds cannot be raptors; one must be sensitive to an animal's comfort and pain; there are directives to provide for the poor and hungry in addition to making sure to feed your domesticated animals before eating yourself. There are even commandments to rest the land every seven days on the Sabbath and every seven years during the *shmitah*. This is done to respect creation and acknowledge the Creator, for we are only hired hands on the rotating Sky Farm below.

### *Mouth*

Mouth is the primary instrument of eating. As in lovemaking, it is a sensual devouring of the other, the swollen red rung lips miming genitalia, passionate mistress to love's arousal, feeding desperate hunger in search of pleasured release. The woman's Lower Mouth—through which life enters and departs—is impregnated by the Rising Sun in which she is initiated as both Holy Whore and Matron of Life, as Temple of Birth itself. She is ground and being, one who suffers so that life may emerge. Among the many symbolic meanings of the Oroboros is that it mimics the cyclical rhythm of procreation: The tail is reminiscent of phallus while the snake's mouth is the receptive vaginal canal.

The mouth is a many-mastered thing: It can laugh, whistle, gargle and eat; speak in every language and sing in every song. It can also remain silent and closed, a sentry between inside and out, rejecter of censored words and forbidden foods. Garlanded by elastic lips, equipped with ivory clad teeth, bordered by hard and soft palates and featuring agile tongue, it is Mile Zero of the Alimentary Highway. From mouth to anus, desire to dust, the mouth contributes to digestion—teeth masticate, salivary glands dispense secretions, tongue adds taste buds, licks and assists swallowing while lips grasp, suction, slurp and smack. The mouth is mother of language, treasury of *logos* and carrier of breath. It is also cave of creation as when Yahweh spoke the world into existence or when the toddler Krishna mischievously ate clay and his mother Yashoda pried open his mouth where she saw the entire universe within.

### *World Tree*

World Tree is *axis mundi,* navel, and *omphalos,* the universal spine that extends through all realms. Occasionally depicted as inverted with roots in Heaven and branches brushing the Earth below, a variant is the Philosophical Tree of the *Opus Magnum* whose offshoots support dissolving and binding powers,[76] topped by the tripartite crowns of the three realms—vegetable, animal and mineral. The Tree encourages diversity—the multi-patinated coat of survival—and then unifies it just the same. It is both transcendent and immanent, one whose fruit nurtures all and whose canopy shelters those who take refuge beneath its spreading garland. It is graced with supernal dew and roots of eternity, with divine messages communicated through the *ruah*-rustled leaves of Spirit Breath that stirs creation from its dream into awakened quintessence.

The Earth is a forest of Cosmic Trees—the birch, banyan, oak and ash; redwood, cedar, laurel and fir; the plum, fig, almond and olive; the Linden, Yggdrasil, Bodhi and the Cross. Each nation champions its arbour; each climate knows its soul. Not only do these trees provide symbolic spiritual values but also sustenance, light, medicine, fuel and building material. They partake of fecund female and potent male characteristics, incarnations of Mother Earth and Father Sky, Triple Goddess and Father Phallus, Wizened Witch and her Old Man. *Yang* and its *yin* are omnipresent partners in a dramatic *pas de deux* of hard and soft, delicate and gnarled, waxing and waning, yielding and resisting, the one because of the other and the other because of the One.

Other great trees that were pleasing to the eye and good for food were planted in the east of Eden, in the paradigmatic Garden of Earthly Delights. All were permitted to those first sentient humans except for the berried branches of two trees in the midst of the enigmatic garden—the Greenwood of Life and the Tree of the Knowledge of Good and Evil. The primeval couple were warned, "When you eat from it you will surely die." And die they did, transformed from one state of consciousness to be reborn into another.

We insist on recapitulating this etiological narrative, for just as they were driven out of an idealized Paradise our present world has begun to vomit[77] us out of its injured habitat as a consequence of our noxious actions. The Tree of Life in the centre of the garden has begun to wilt under our incessant assault, a consequence of our insatiable appetite to consume. We have become a tyrannical, difficult to control Oroboros whose head compulsively yearns for its nourishing tail. At least the original archetypal Dragon still adheres to a series of balancing principles whereas we have bruised the serpent and disturbed the unifying order.

We, too, now retreat into an exile where we eat bread by the sweat of our overheated brow and where we increasingly find ourselves in a disjointed world that if it is not beset by drought then it is drowning in floodwaters. A mass species extinction looms while we heedlessly feast on the fruits of our over-zealous labours. We have monetized nature, anointed industrialized landscapes and charred forests with the burning tears of the unfortunate casualties of our greed. Aztec-like, we have eviscerated virgin hearts in imagined appeasement to commercial harvest gods.

The World Tree, however, *will* prevail for we are just temporary denizens of a distant planet making its obedient rounds here in the oceanic bosom of enduring metaspace.

### *Cosmic Egg*

The seed and the egg are symbols of eternal resurrection. Humbly swaddled in terra's incubating cradle—within Mother of All Life's dedicated womb or beneath the nested body of patient parents—they grow into embryonic life. They also tell the story of "that which must be broken in order to be whole." The seed cannot fully germinate unless it breaks its jacket, pushes up as it sprouts, breaches the soil ceiling to leave the underworld and emerge into an alternate sphere of light. Similarly, the ovarian vault of the fertilized egg is nursery to insect, reptile, bird and fish until it, too, must be shattered in the service of life.

And then there is the broken heart that opens in pain and deepens to character. The Orphic Poems—the mysteries of ancient Greek lore—tell of Night as she who was in the beginning a black-winged oracular bird. Inseminated by the Wind she laid a silver egg in the Ocean of Darkness from which Eros, the golden god of love, was born. These are the stories that may never have literally happened and yet are eternally recurring as the Drama of the Cosmic Egg described in ancient world mythologies.

Contemporary physicists speculate that fourteen billion years ago the universe was compressed into a gravitational singularity—a world egg—from which it explosively hatched and is still expanding. One day, it, too, will collapse upon itself as it has so many times before in the circuit of universal respiration. What interests me, however, is what preceded the First Breath and what will follow the Last. All issues of sustenance dwell within the parentheses of those vast questions.

### *The Empyreal Wars*

I wonder if one day the gods and their priests will be satisfied. If one day hunger will be sated so that there would no longer be ceremonial cooking in cauldrons of flesh to celebrate symbolic holy days. If one day there will be no need for this endless sacrifice of life for the sake of life; no fodder because no hunger. I wonder if one day there will be a death of birth and its perpetual struggle to survive; if all will return to its origin or arrive at its destination (a place where there is no space), in a time beyond counting. (Time is also a commodity, for it, too, can be measured and expended even as it constantly swallows us whole.) I wonder if one day there will finally be a reconciliation with the Empyreal Wars of Creation.

Meanwhile, existence persists as a feeding frenzy like the old Earth Lady who swallowed a spider to catch the fly, perhaps she'll die. These interconnected food chains—Gaia's elegant bionecklace recumbent upon Oroboros's endless neck—with their related trophic levels are woven into larger mutually dependent webs. Plants and algae absorb nutrients from their environment and also produce their own food; herbivores—primary consumers—eat plants; predators hunt and eat them; carnivores that eat other carnivores occupy the fourth level. Apex predators, such as lions and humans, are at the top of the chain. Decomposers, like bacteria and fungi, feast on dead matter converting it back into nutrients for primary producers. The process continues under various disguises in every particle of existence from the air we breathe to massive galactic cannibals that have been digesting their last celestial meal for a billion years. Some even say there is a restaurant at the end of the universe.[78]

It took thousands of generations of experimentation and accidental discovery to determine what was edible: Some things could be eaten raw while others had to be cooked; some were avoided as poison while others became daily staples or occasional luxuries. Some products—opium poppy, peyote cactus, cannabis, psilocybin mushroom, Ayahuasca jungle brew and the vine of Bacchus[79]—were regarded as magical, medicinal, sacred or forbidden. Some nourished the body, others the mind—a soul source to spirit dreams and prophetic visions, mythic manna, shaman's wings or the addict's prison. Injected, ingested, smoked or drunk, they are purveyors of synesthesial perceptions, psychedelic tickets to the Heart of Heaven, a meal in the presence of the Sapphire Throne, face to face with Divine Madness. While some of these substances were tolerated, then prohibited and finally permitted-under-advisory for recreational use, others were deemed destructive to societies and death sentences to individual users. They became controlled substances, banned as illicit stimulants, forbidden fruit craved by the ever-agitated human mind.

The sapiens species has two mouths to feed: Its corporeal body and its conscious spirit that has evolved—according to our conceits—in the Image of the Gods. We belong to Heaven as much as to

Earth and have appetite for one as much as the other. We yearn to escape the chains of unbearable limitations, to dance at the Gates of Infinity just beyond the portal to the Valley of Ten Thousand Winds. Yet we remain fragile creatures and sometimes, like Icarus, fall from enchanted heights to mundane realities, even martyrdom, below.

### *Destination*

We end where we began in the clasp of serpent circle, eating—and being eaten—our way through the universe. There is no judgment in the Archetypal Kingdom of Oroboros from which I've emerged just long enough to tell you this strange tale. *Es, es, mein kynd,*[80] for the journey is long and littered with obstacles.[81] On the day you arrive you will no longer recognize yourself[82] for if you did it would be a sign that you have not yet reached your true destination.

*This essay appeared in a somewhat different form in "Sustenance: Writers from BC and Beyond on the Subject of Food" (Anvil Press 2017), edited by Rachel Rose. – Ed.*

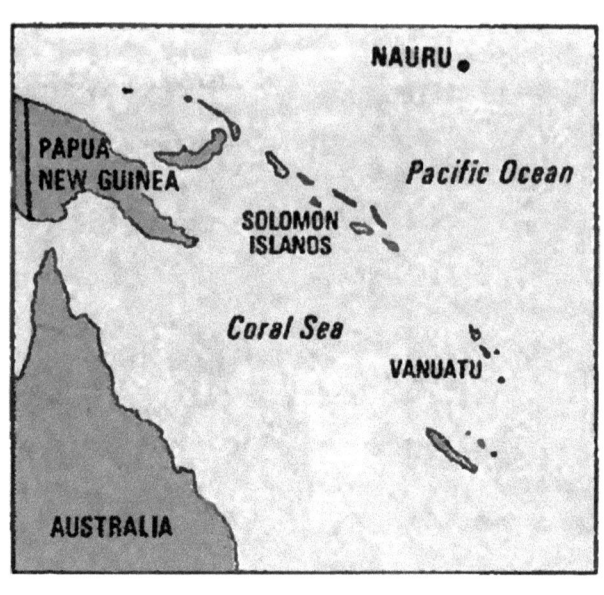

# REFLECTIONS UPON TURNING SEVENTY

*March 8-11, 2019*
*Sailing north aboard the MS Amsterdam on the Coral Sea in the Great Barrier Reef Marine Park along the northeast coast of Australia, the land of Down Under...*

In less than three weeks, on Tuesday, March 26, 2019, I will celebrate my 70th birthday. Hundreds of millions of people have been there before but for me it will be the first and last time (unless theories of reincarnation are actually true and not just convenient theological placebos).

Two friends reminded me of a grammatical time illusion: Except for one's first day of birth, the birthday celebration is actually the *completion* of the past year. During one's first year of existence we say that the baby is six weeks old, or three or eight months old. It is "one year old" only after 365 days and counting.[83] I am, therefore, not in my 69th year but nearing the completion of my seventieth. The birthday will also mark the beginning of the seventy-first year. Not as complicated as the International Date Line but pretty close.

As I approach this milestone I feel the stirring of a number of emotional reactions. I remember being at a *Melavah Malka,* a post-Shabbat ceremony, on Mount Zion in Jerusalem when I was a student there in the early 1970s. Someone who I did not know was celebrating his seventieth birthday that night and so we drank a *le'chaim* to him. I remember his words, at first somewhat strange, but never forgotten: "Seventy years," he said, "is a long time to look forward to but a short time to look back upon."[84]

Seventy years, however, is only a long time relative to an average human life span. Conversely, some organisms only live a few hours while there are stars that exist for billions of years. Jewish tradition instructs us to bless one another to live a full 120 years. This is derived from two sources: The first is *Genesis* 6:3—"Then the Lord said, 'My Spirit shall not abide in man forever, for he is flesh: his days shall be 120 years.'" The second is from Moses who lived to that age: "Moses was a hundred and twenty years old when he died, yet his eyes were not weak and his vitality had not diminished" (*Deut.* 34:7). Ironically, the latest scientific estimation for the maximum human biological life span is also 120 years.

### *Time: The True Luxury*

As we age, time becomes the greatest luxury. To help appreciate the value of time, imagine that every minute and each mile calculated below is equivalent to a dollar. Spend them wisely.

*Some approximate statistics gleaned from various sources and my imperfect calculations*

70 is 7 x 10. The number seventy could be understood as 7 representing *time* (as in seven days in a week), multiplied by 10, that is the ten fingers on our hands, i.e. the fullness of human *action*. Seventy is

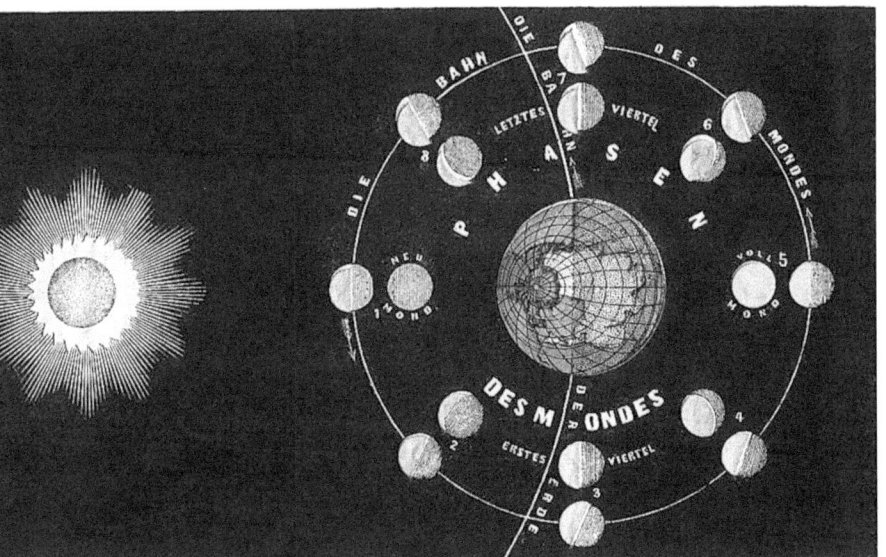

Detail from a 19th century German book illustration, "Transparente Darstellung der Mondsphasen," depicting the relative movements of the earth, moon and sun.

therefore time multiplied by action embraced by space. It is potential realized; kinetic energy actualized.

- Number of minutes in a day: 1440.
- Number of minutes in a year: 525,600.
- Number of minutes in seventy years: 36,792,000.

This is how far we travel just by remaining in any one spot on our planet:

- Distance travelled in a day as the Earth *rotates* eastward (at a speed of approximately 1,000 mph) on its axis: 25,000 miles. In addition, our planet travels another 1.6 million miles a day at an orbital speed of 67,000 mph as it *revolves* around the sun.

- Distance travelled in a year as Earth rotates on its axis: 9,125,000 miles.

- Distance travelled in a year as the Earth orbits the Sun: 584 million miles.

- Distance travelled by the Earth as part of the solar system that, in turn, orbits around the galactic centre of the Milky Way is another 4.5 billion miles per year.

- In addition, the galaxy itself is moving through the universe.

- Furthermore, the local cluster of galaxies is in motion relative to the Cosmic Background Radiation.

- And, we have been told, the Universe is still expanding [into what?]. Perhaps at the end of this *exhalation* there will be an *inhalation* until all matter and time are severely condensed and then propelled, once again, into the next Big Bang. But who or what is Master of the Cosmic Breath? Is there more than just one universe? Where did it come from; where is it going? Is all this purely mechanistic or does it have meaning and purpose?

- The total of all movements—travelling at a combined speed of many hundreds of thousands of miles an hour—is approximately 15.5 billion miles (25 billion km) per year and probably a great deal more.

Those are just the physical global movements of Spaceship Earth. Even if you were to remain perfectly still you would be considered a Frequent Flyer racking up over fifteen billion miles each year.

Add to that the movement *within* the body such as respiration, cell locomotion and blood circulation. Each person takes approximately 20,000 breaths every day; 7.5 million per year. The heart beats about 100,000 times a day and 35 million times in a year as it propels our blood 12,000 miles each day through the body. This constant busyness for the sake of maintaining life in the average person is in addition to another kind of travel: The *movement of mind—*

what the Buddhists refer to as "monkey mind," the restless reverberations caused by our passions and desires, real or imagined.⁸⁵ A constant imperative orchestrates the universe and we, whether we want to or not, have been swept up in the cosmic dance.

### *One species among many; various life expectancies*
I don't feel as attached to our species, *Homo sapiens*, as much as I used to. I consider us a quickly evolving species that exhibits both the best and the worst of characteristics.⁸⁶ Where else can you find the personification of evil one moment and an expression of gentle tenderness the next? This radical juxtaposition of divergent principles that unfold under the constant critical commentary of a judicious consciousness is rather unique in this corner of the universe. Although I will cling to humanity for as long as possible, I feel even more rooted in cosmological time, in Time out of Mind, and even more at home in the Hearth of Heaven.

There are times, however, when I feel immense love and compassion for everything—living or inert—that exists (although I still sometimes suffer from frustration and anger, most often directed at other people). I smile every year after the Winter thaw when magnolias unfurl their pink-tinged temporary flowers. And I welcome the return of the first flies of Spring—buzzing creatures with five eyes and eight thousand lenses—who will be my hungry housemates for the next six months.

Some species of insects (which are also classified as animals), such as the mayfly, may live for only a few hours or a single day. The adult's primary function is reproduction; it doesn't even take time to feed. Other animals inhabit their domain for over a hundred and fifty years.

The average life expectancy for some species depends on their function. Worker bees, for example, live for 5 to 6 weeks in the Summer. During the Winter, however, a typical worker's life is extended for up to six months so it can fulfill its functions of sustaining the hive and raising new workers for the next Spring. Queen honeybees have been known to live from 2 to 5 years. Termites typically live 1 to 2 years but termite queens may live up to 50 years. House flies average 15 to 25 days. Some parrots live 80 years while the giant tortoise—Eastern symbol of wisdom and longevity—lumbers about for 150 years. Our pet dogs' life expectancies vary according to size and breed (8 to 15 years), while pet cats live 12 to 18 years.

Plants range from single cell organisms to giant redwood sequoias and live from a few weeks to thousands of years.

The Earth is about 4.5 billion years old; the Sun a bit more, the Moon somewhat less. Geologic time defines mountains and rocks, tectonic plates, subterranean rivers, volcanoes and the Earth's mantle that she wears as a cloak around her molten core. Each element of geology passes through various phases: Are the waters not ruled by different laws and measured by liquid clocks that determine whether a collection of water will present itself as a day puddle or an ancient ocean, a swollen river of melted snow or a dried desert bed? "All rivers run to the sea, but the sea is never full; from the place from which the streams come, there they flow again."[87]

When contemplating my own corporeal demise here on this swiftly tilting planet, I realize anything that exists at all is a kind of miracle. What are the astronomical odds of any one of us being born in the first place? I once asked that question to a friend, Jonathan Berkowitz, who is a professor of statistics at UBC, a puzzler and World Backward Spelling Champion. He said that there were too many variables to consider and that it was impossible to calculate. When I protested, he paraphrased Groucho Marx, saying: "If you don't like my conclusions, I have others."[88]

## *Many types of time*

Time is a river without banks, a Great River that contains all the others. There are many ways to measure this flow of time and many types of time to measure. In the midst of all these chronologies in this grand shop of ticking clocks, each type of time wears its own mask, has its own texture and is draped in its peculiar uniform. Some are modest, ancient and wise while others are boisterous, insistent and impetuous; some are elegant and reserved, others clumsy or bold; some disappear in camouflage while others celebrate their audacity and live by a different set of rules.

There is clock time that strictly adheres to its objectively measured functions and then there is subjective time, that which is gauged more as an emotional perception of what it felt like. There is rodent[89] or fish time—like all of us, we may live out our lives or unexpectedly be captured by predators or be cut short by disease or misfortune. There is ephemeral steam from a kitchen's cooking alchemy as water transforms from liquid to gas, or gradually condenses to a solid in the freezer. The genesis of an individual or a nation is trumpeted by the painful moment of birth, while death, the end of a brief and almost meaningless life, is often similarly bedecked in suffering and mourning. Existence emerges and disappears in the unforgiving crucible of time.

## *Speculations on the nature of reality*

Entering my eighth decade of exploring existence, I have still not achieved any certainty concerning most of the really big questions. Even some master physicists declare that we will never understand everything. My convictions, however, are that although we may not understand the mysteries of the universe at present, one day we will. Our questions imply the answers. If we can imagine such queries it must mean that the Universe is attempting to communicate with us but we have not yet learned how to discern its responses.

Here is what I theorize at this point: these are the questions I ask and the answers I contemplate. God, Transcendent Numinosity or secular Eternity, fills [and yet is also separate from] the Spacetime Continuum and serves as host to all that ever was, is or will be. Some speak about this Deity creating *ex nihilo*—"something from nothing," or at least imposing order on the *Tohu Va'Vohu*, the tumultuous mix of Chaos, confusion and emptiness. Then (after a parenthetical existence of trillions of years) everything will return to its original state of non-existence. We live in that parenthesis between creation and dissolution; we are temporary denizens of the Grand Illusion. According to these speculations, only the Creative Force exists before, during and after time/space materiality. Although mystical literature is filled with speculation as to "why," only the Force might know why it felt compelled to impose creation upon a previously non-existent cosmos.[90]

Or is all existence without meaning? Does suffering have no significance and labour no love? Have we—from infant to stardust and from great personal kindness to indifferent black hole—been victims of some capricious Immortal's whim, one who decided to engage in a cosmic Arts & Crafts Project and ended up with the world as we know it? Have we been both created and violated by a Universe that was, itself, forced into existence? Don't tell me that "God is Love," that God is all good, that God has a reason for everything and it is only for us to believe, accept and worship such an unfathomable deity. These may be comforting thoughts for those who are suffering but are they true, verifiable, irrefutable?

I can no longer simply *believe*. I want, I (respectfully) demand, to *know*. And I want a *Numen* that wants to be known in return. Nothing personal here; please just reveal the Glory[91](*Kavod*), the Way[92] (*Derekh*) and the Face[93] (*Panim*). But now, suddenly, I am reminded that Moses made a similar request on the Desert Mountain that had already been the scene of so much divine drama: The Burning Bush, seeing Thunder and hearing Lightning, the Pillar of Fire and Clouds of Glory, giving of the Ten Commandments and revelation of the One God while, at its base camp, the frightened neophytes were busy sculpting the Golden Calf.

After disappointing yet understandable theatrics from the newly liberated slave nation, and when it seemed like everything was about to fall apart, Moses negotiated on behalf of the doomed people. He may have broken the Two Tablets in exasperation but he also climbed the mountain again to request a second edition. This time, more familiar with *Ehyeh* (or *Yahweh* of Many Names[94]), he also wanted to know more about the reality of who was directing him. He was told, *Lo yir'aini ha'adam ve'hai*, "No one can see me and live." But he was still granted more than most of us could bear: Protected by stone cavern and divine hand he was given a glimpse of the retreating back.[95] And it was enough—*dayeinu*.

I, too, may have to die to my desire-to-know so that I might comprehend in another way. As Zalman Schachter-Shalomi once taught "You don't have to wait until you die in order to be resurrected. You can experience multiple non-corporeal deaths and be resurrected again in this lifetime. Each reincarnation offers a potential *aliyah* (ascent), a vehicle with which to continue the journey and arrive at the next *madraiga* (level)."[96] Perhaps that is a reason why I search and study, travel and reinvent myself so that I may build on the past and be reborn to the next level of perception.

From the mountain I see a bird—a great feathered eagle—carrying the nation upon its back.[97] I, too, am transported to Dreamtime, wading in the spilled ink of ancient chronicles when the sky gardens were being filled with stars, the oceans with waters and the first animals roamed the still nascent planet. There is Raven followed by Dove, black braided with white, as creator and then again as trickster, herald of peace. And here is Phoenix ascending from Phyre, when the cycle of destruction is complete and becomes fertile ground once again.

But was this dualistic cycle necessary in the First Place? It was through Creation that confusion entered the universe. Before that, I imagine Dr. Deity perfectly sanguine, complete in Itself and needing no other. Why did it will a physical manifestation of Self? Why did it not only allow but even invite evil, pain and suffering to the prom? Is the Universe as planned or an accidental mutation? But even mutations have their roles to play and seem to be part of the evolutionary cast.

Or perhaps I'm too obsessed with a God Character as the lead actor in the *dramatis personae*. Perhaps there was no creator and no god. Just a series of elemental forces that met one another in the Cosmic Soup of Accidental Recipes, cooked in the cauldron of Indeterminable Time, who became progenitors of organisms and tellers of tales.

Perhaps there is meaning; maybe not. After seventy years of study and searching, of asking questions and performing rituals, of daring to climb too high and descending to claustrophobic depths, after decades of dancing and then sitting still, of calling out and then listening for the echoed answer in simple silence, *I still don't know*. No one does although many have substituted belief for knowledge. The real answers lay in kingdoms beyond the reach of knowledge, beyond the power of words to describe them. No one can direct you there; there may not even be a "there" there. In addition, you will have to leave your singular self behind and allow your non-self to become thoroughly lost. There are no maps.; only the most-subtle of hints suggest the way. But it exists until it doesn't, until suddenly you've arrived.

I can't be satisfied by statements—even by some brilliant scientists—that we will never, can never, know the full extent of the universe or all its operating principles. It may take us another thousand or hundred thousand years, but I am confident that we—as conscious, curious, creative and disciplined explorers of all that exists—

will discover them. My head hurts from banging against the limitations of physical space let alone against the vastness of metaphysical speculation. I want to look beyond the obvious, pass to the other side of tomorrow. Infinity may, by definition, always extend one step beyond the greatest number but I want to transcend infinity even if there is *NoThing* there.

I'm reminded of a conversation I had with my father fifty years ago. I was 21 years old, had just graduated from university, was working as a janitor and living in a one-room walk-up rental in an older house not far from the beach. With no definite plans for the future, my father was concerned about me so we went for a walk and talk on the beach. As the tide was coming in he asked about my plans. Because I didn't want to give him a superficial answer I was silent for a moment and then responded with something that surprised even me. "The goalless goal," I heard myself say, something I'd read in a book on Zen Buddhism. "That is my goal, that is my destination." Of course it made no sense to him and I may have been stalling for time, but it was as deep a truth as I've ever spoken.

I've discovered that the rational mind armed with its arsenal of words, numbers and concepts can only take us so far. I want to pass beyond time and transcend space but that is a journey upon which the confines of this body cannot embark. I will therefore have to board a different vehicle, that of Imagination, in order to arrive at my destination. There may be other ways but I am not yet a skilled enough cosmonaut, a sailor among the unchartered mysteries.

### *Aging transformations of body and soul*

As I get older I reluctantly notice transformations in my body and changes in my perceptions. My hair gets thinner as my belly gets thicker; my strength lessens and breath shortens even as my sight dims but vision deepens. My patience grows short and my memory long;

I cry more and am easily provoked but just as often don't really care; I laugh more fully but tragedy insulates me from the innocence of my youth; I walk slower and mostly for exercise whereas I used to walk as fast as I can now run and then I had a thousand important places to go. I enjoy gardens whereas I used to be impatient with the time it took for things to grow; I choose my battles and have abandoned most wars; I dedicate more time to writing because the always promised "someday" has come and gone even as I rush to reclaim what few embers still remain. Mortality is my teacher; doctors my priests. As each day becomes rarer I regard them as more precious and strive to turn the remnants of my dreams into vibrant, or even ordinary, realities.

In a further attempt to be self-reflective, over the past two years I also spent time reviewing my life and how I've interacted with others. That involved patiently reviewing family archives—organizing and culling tens of thousands of pages, letters, photographs, notebooks and mementoes. Many were eventually recycled but most were respectfully placed in large plastic bins. Each family member's memories are now organized and accessible. It took about a dozen bins and boxes to gather my archives including journals and business records, as well as teenage love letters and correspondence with others over the years. I also had documents attesting to places I lived, schools I attended, places I worked and communities I served. This exercise evoked many emotional reactions:

- what if I had remained with that person?
- tears of regret
- communications requesting forgiveness
- gratitude for various experiences
- and, finally, an acceptance of life as it is.

The Talmud suggests that someone who learns but does not review is comparable to one who plants but then fails to harvest.[98] The same is true for life in general.

## *Reflections on aging from biblical and rabbinic literature*

YW designed this bookmark when serving as rabbi
at Temple Shalom, Medford, Massachusetts (1986-1991)

Below are a few quotes from biblical and rabbinic literature about aging. There are many more. Each one bears multiple levels of interpretation: some literal; others symbolic. The Kabbalah speaks about *Hamishim Sha'arei Binah*—Fifty Gates of Wisdom, and the Midrash introduces the idea of *Shivim Panim Le'Torah*—Seventy Facets to the Torah. When exploring the cosmos as well as the Essence behind the Purdah, one becomes appreciative of as many sources of interpretive knowledge as possible. You never know what key will unlock the door before you.

> *Genesis 5:1-32*
> This is the book of the generations of Adam. When God created man, he made him in the likeness of God. Male and female he created them, and he blessed them and named them human when they were created. When Adam had lived 130 years, he fathered a son in his own likeness, after his image, and named him Seth. The days of Adam after he fathered Seth were 800 years; and he had other sons and daughters. Thus all the days that Adam lived were 930 years, and he died.

*Genesis* 6:3
Then the Lord said, "My Spirit shall not abide in man forever, for he is flesh: his days shall be 120 years."

*Psalm* 90:10
The years of our life are seventy or, even by reason of strength, eighty; yet their span is but toil and trouble; they are soon gone, and we fly away.

*Psalm* 90:1–17
A Prayer of Moses, the man of God. Lord, you have been our dwelling place in all generations. Before the mountains were brought forth, or ever you had formed the earth and the world, from everlasting to everlasting you are God. You return people to dust and say, "Return, O children of man!" For a thousand years in your sight are but as yesterday when it is past, or as a watch in the night. You sweep them away as with a flood; they are like a dream, like grass that is renewed in the morning.

*Proverbs* 16:31
Gray hair is a crown of glory; it is gained in a righteous life.

*Job* 14:5
Since his days are determined, and the number of his months is with you, and you have appointed his limits that he cannot pass.

*Pirkei Avot* 5:22
Reb Yehudah ben Teima used to say: At five years of age a person should study the Scriptures, at ten years the Mishnah, at 13 the Commandments, and at 15 the Talmud; at 18 he should get married, 20 is the age for one's life pursuit, 30 is the age for authority, 40 for discernment, 50 is the age for giving counsel, 60 is the time to be an elder, 70 for gray hair; 80 is the age for special strength, at 90 for decrepitude, and

at 100 a person is as one who has already died and has ceased from the affairs of this world.

*Zohar Breisheet* 91b
There is a *midrash*, a teaching story, that tells of God speaking with Adam in the Garden of Eden. The Prime Mover caused a mist to arise from the Earth on which he projected all the future generations of the first man's genealogy. At one point Adam noticed a baby being born but then dying. He asked the Creator who the child might have been if he had survived, to which God responded: "He would have grown to become David, King and Sweet Singer of Israel. He would have been the great ancestor of the fulfillment of human destiny, the Messiah." Adam then asked God if he could give that child a gift of seventy of his years. The Creator told him that his request would be granted this one time but never repeated so that henceforth everyone was destined to live his allotted years, not more and not less. Whereupon David was gifted with seventy years[99] and Adam's life was 930, not 1,000, years.

There are other concepts I'd like to discuss[100] but will have to leave them for another time, perhaps when I return from my distant journey.

***Search for the essence of existence and fulfilling life's challenges***
As we age and look back upon our lives, how many of our imagined aspirations were fulfilled and how many did we have to abandon gracefully or with some regret?[101] When I was younger—a process that began when I was about six and continued through my twenties—and started to perceive the outside world, I wanted to achieve all that was humanly possible in the physical, intellectual, spiritual and emotional realms.

- *Physically,* I wanted to be an Olympian (those were the days when the Olympics were still relegated to amateur athletics) and then play professional sports. In this world of action I wanted to be able to do anything that I desired, to be well-known and to become a philanthropist in order to assist others achieve their goals.

- *Intellectually,* I wanted to become the smartest person or one of the most knowledgeable people in the world.

- *Spiritually,* I craved enlightenment; wanted to be bathed in the essence of universal consciousness; to be a psychic and healer.

- *Emotionally,* I wanted to embrace kindness, to tremble with love and intuit the heart of the other.

As I review these desires, in retrospect it seems like I had a rather active ego but I did not consider myself an arrogant person. I remained somewhat introverted as one who struggled with emotional issues. I was involved in sports but was never a star athlete, and although I did my best in school I never achieved the intellectual faculties that I recognized in others. I was, however, dedicated to fulfilling the gift of life so what was lacking in natural abilities was made up through determination.

Growing up, I knew I was Jewish. I was sent to Talmud Torah elementary school; we kept mostly kosher at home with two sets of dishes and kosher meat; we had a *pushke* (charity box) in the cupboard and contributed to numerous causes; our family attended the orthodox Schara Tzedeck *shul*; I went to Camp Hatikvah every summer and my parents belonged to community organizations.

Privately, however, I was somewhat embarrassed to be a MOT (Member of the Tribe). That was probably because of subtle emotional messages I received from my parents who, as children, had to escape the antisemitic pogroms of Eastern Europe. My father's family emigrated from Odessa in 1928, exactly in the middle of the inter-war years. He and his brother were almost killed in two separate attacks by the marauding Cossacks; my grandfather barely escaped with his life. My mother's family left Pinsk, Poland for Edmonton around the same time. Most of those who remained behind perished in the Holocaust.

I developed an unconscious visceral cognition that I carried in my bones. As a defense mechanism—emotional as much as physical—I learned to hide. I still look over my shoulder and make quick, almost casual, escape plans from almost every situation. You cannot really know me because if you did I would be discovered and might die. Consequently, I've spent most of my life hiding in plain sight. I dare not even see myself too clearly for fear of being both caught and simultaneously disappearing.

In an effort to know myself and achieve my rather pregnant agenda, I studied comparative religions and mythologies, burned incense and practiced meditations, experimented with drugs both Earth-born and chemically compounded, was shy around people but familiar with gods and their pantheon of ambassadors. I went to therapy time and again, often reluctantly but fuelled with hope, to deal with issues the shadow of which still abides. I was blessed with my father's emotional and financial support so that I could travel[102] and search the world for teachers[103] in forests or Holy Cities, in mountain monasteries or in red brick Ivy League schools, in rustic sanctuaries or urban spiritual communities.

I also became familiar with darkness, approached madness as an escape from life's too many responsibilities, confused sex for love and camped in hotel slums as a relief from respectability. I lived in the most basic dormitories on threadbare mattresses over stiff steel springs covered by thin wool blankets so I would not have to waste time taking care of an apartment and could be minutes away from the halls of study. Later, I was able to tutor others, then teach, but I was always learning whether from books or classes, from guides or nature, from everything and all. Mostly from my own mistakes. And still I feel as empty as the vast vacuum of space.

There were decades of chanting and praying, turning pages and beating hearts, watching breath and calming thought, changing names[104] and drinking dew, silent retreats and intoxicated song. To rendezvous with different shades of divinity, I've risen in the dark of day before the sun lifted Aurora's golden veil and studied late into the night until diamond-studded stars faded into dawn's pillowed crypt. I've feasted and fasted, had good food and none at all, tried exotic and cleansing diets, was obsessed with sex and dated by the dozen, became a student of the body as well as the mind, and learned healing techniques emanating from the ancient East as well as the classical and contemporary West. Teachings tumbled from the Old World and the New Age in equal measure.

In due course, I also shared what I learned and became a teacher for thousands of students from pre-school through university and adult education, although I still don't really know what it's all about. I became a rabbi only as a technique to force myself to continue learning. I've performed too many funerals and not enough weddings, visited hospitals, prisons and asylums, and cried in broken homes of sorrowful mourning when there was nothing else one could do.

Rudolph Otto described encountering the Numen as the *mysterium tremendum et fascinans,* an experience that is at once mysterious, terrifying and urgent as well as endlessly fascinating. In my search for this Universal Essence it seemed that all I had to do was to follow the shadow to reveal the source. I was gradually humbled, however, by the dichotomy of being human. We may conceive of eternity but can only manage a few decades; we may appreciate empyreal power but can only manipulate minor mechanics; we may perceive the fullness of cosmic presence, even transcend its theoretical limitations, but can only transmit our limited being over inconsequential acreage.

And so as I limp home like Jacob after wrestling with the angel, I realize that even if I live to the statistical average life span in our culture of 80 years old (for men; about 84 for women), I only have ten years left. On the other hand I could go tomorrow or stretch it for another couple of decades. Will I crumble, wilt, or panic under the "death sentence" as I enter one of the final chapters in my life? We've all admired the NFL quarterback who can rally his team under almost impossible odds, needing a touchdown to win with ninety yards to go and less than two minutes on the clock. I identify with that scenario as I begin the final drive. I'm glad to be on your team, to share your company, to be your friend. An ally.

### Wednesday, March 20, 2019
### *A Purim Blessing*

After a long labour, my mother gave birth to me on March 26th, 1949, corresponding to the 25th of *Adar*, a Shabbat between *Purim* and *Pesah* on the Jewish calendar. I've appreciated the rebirthing of Spring ever since. I found myself an Aries, the ram, a fire and first sign of the zodiac. Renewal is in my blood; my first breath was filled with blossoms. I'm a practical optimist. It isn't just a question of half empty or half full: If I'm thirsty, I'll pick it up and drink.

A few evenings ago, on Purim, about twenty Jewish people gathered in the Hudson Room on the MS *Amsterdam*. Some of us dressed up in costumes; at least an amusing hat. The onboard rabbi (there is also a priest and minister) read an abridged *Megillat Esther* (Scroll of Esther) and spoke about the holiday. We sang a Purim song, drank wine and ate some *hamantaschen* pastries. I brought a cold bottle of Absolut Vodka Citron and encouraged those who wanted to partake to join in drinking a *le'chaim*. After most people left, a few of us remained behind for another drink or three and to dig into the *hamantaschen* that had been especially baked by the onboard Asian pastry chef who also bakes us fresh challah every Friday evening for *Oneg Shabbat*.

I especially connected with two men: Joseph, 81, who, as a child, had survived the Holocaust in Holland; the other, Herb, 84, was a pony-tailed American whose wife passed away five years ago and who met his present wife in that same room on a cruise last year. With a mixture of tears that only fall when one recognizes a twin soul, and with alcohol-infused broken hearts, we shared stories about our Polish and Russian families, about pogroms and the *Shoah*. I revealed to them that I was somewhat concerned about turning seventy in a few days. They both smiled and rebuffed my fears with heartfelt encouragement, insisting that "You are still young!" "Enjoy life. You still have so much to live for!" They were sincere. I paused for a moment, abandoned my resistance and believed them. [I slept in the next day until 2 p.m. recovering from my inebriated flight of fancy.]

I now know that their words were a Purim *brakhah*, a blessing against all odds uttered on Noah's Ark drifting in Indonesian waters, a transmission from strangers, these two landsmen I suddenly realized I had known all my life. Although I still value my solitude, tonight I appreciated friendship more than ever. I think of my friends back home and wish them good health, positive attitudes and gratifying accomplishments. I pray that they, too, may be blessed with pleasant companionship, a meaningful life and manna from heaven.

I sign off with these words as I sit in the ship's library with the requisite fine wood and brass tables complimented by a large floor-standing globe. Some people are reading books or immersed in their electronic devices, one woman is knitting, another studying an atlas and two men are locked in a chess match. In the adjacent Explorer's Lounge a violin and piano duo are playing Viennese waltzes and other popular music. Some passengers listen lightly while others, older than me, still dance with a surprisingly joyful elegance. The Ocean Orchestra plays on as notes fall effortlessly from their well-rehearsed sleeves.

I could add to these contemplations but in order to share them with you I must let them go. Perhaps that, too, is an analogy for the Autumn of our lives: Learning to observe the slow, inevitable, changes that announce themselves so imperceptibly; to strengthen ourselves where we can and let go when we must. No wisdom here; just dust in the ever-whirling wind.

### *March 25, 2019*

Three weeks have passed since I began writing reflections on the upcoming birthday milestone. I suppose I was experiencing some anxiety in finally accepting "the seventy" and so delayed completing my thoughts. Since then we sailed to Darwin in northern Australia and then to Komodo Island, Indonesia to visit the mythical Komodo dragons. We continued through the unique Hindu enclave of Bali followed by a pilgrimage to the great Buddhist temple of Borobudur. Then on to Singapore, one of the great city-states in the world today, before passing through the Andaman Sea and into the Bay of Bengal. The warm waters of the Indian Ocean lay just ahead. It is where I will greet my threshold day of reckoning, the completion of seven decades and onto the eighth.

### *March 26, 2019*

After seventy years of uninterrupted labour, the day finally arrived. I recited *Modeh* (the short prayer of gratitude that greets each day), opened one eye and then the next, checked my still-buoyant heart, took a deep breath and carried on. There remains so much more to know, to do, to be. Old Men, I now realize, must still be explorers.

# OLD MEN OUGHT TO BE EXPLORERS

***Introduction***

In October of 2018, Michael Audain and his wife, Yoshiko Karasawa, set out on a pilgrimage to visit the sacred sites of Jerusalem (where he planned to walk in the footsteps of Jesus) and Rome (for an audience with the Pope). Upon hearing of their intentions and moved by Michael's sincerity, I prepared a carefully assembled bundle of offerings for their journey, all meticulously knotted in an antique textile. Among the gifts were books and articles, incense, a soft shoulder bag from Kyoto and other choice presents. I felt like one of the Magi, the Three Wise Men, bearing gifts upon an auspicious occasion. These were accompanied by a letter wishing Michael and Yoshi an inspiring journey and safe travels.

The letter included the prayer poem, *A Sleep of Prisoners,* by the English Quaker playwright, Christopher Fry, originally written in 1951. I had been introduced to the stirring verse by Jean Houston many years before and it was now my turn to pass it on to one who I greatly respected but was still rather intimidated to approach. The immediacy of the moment triumphed and I dared to deliver the treasured package a few days before their departure.

Soon after, I received a deeply sensitive email from Michael that he wrote in the darkest night, among the stars, flying high over the Atlantic on their way to London, the first leg of their journey. He began his letter by quoting from *A Sleep of Prisoners.* The poem had become his anthem and he had already memorized it.

> The human heart can go the lengths of God…
>
> Dark and cold we may be, but this
> Is no winter now. The frozen misery
> Of centuries breaks, cracks, begins to move;
> The thunder is the thunder of the floes,
> The thaw, the flood, the upstart Spring.
>
> Thank God our time is now when wrong
> Comes up to face us everywhere,
> Never to leave us till we take
> The longest stride of soul men ever took.
>
> Affairs are now soul size.
> The enterprise
> Is exploration into God.
> Where are you making for? It takes
> So many thousand years to wake…
> But will you wake, for pity's sake!

I, in turn, was so intensely moved by his devoted and wise words that I felt unworthy of responding.

Here are excerpts from Michael's message:

**From:** Michael Audain
**Subject:** The human heart can go to the lengths of God, Dark and cold we may be, but this is no winter now. The frozen misery of centuries breaks, cracks, begins to move, the thunder of the floes, The thaw, the flood, the upstart Spring.
**Date:** October 25, 2018
**To:** Yosef Wosk

Dear Brother Yosef:
As I fly across the Atlantic en route to Jerusalem the Golden, I read this prayer from "A Sleep of Prisoners" over and over in the early dawn until it became part of me.

The gifts that you have endowed us with are beyond measure. So much wisdom was wrapped up in that beautiful blue shawl in which they were enfolded. I immediately read your elegant commencement addresses knowing that no one else in our town could speak so beautifully about art and quote so aptly from both the Judaic and Christian texts.

Yoshi was also thrilled with the Japanese shoulder bag for which she sincerely thanks you and intends to carry around the holy places on our journey east.

I have to tell you though, Yosef, that I feel so unworthy of your kindness and attention as I am really just a poor sinner who is making this trip in the hope that praying in the very places where Christ Jesus was born, lived, taught and died will somewhat help me repent so that my many sins may be washed clean.

The fact that we will be calling at Rome on the way back for a blessing may also help. I keep remembering though that the Holy Father is my age and himself a prisoner of a huge institution which itself needs to repent for its great sins of commission and omission...

my ancestors having had to flee France in the late 17th century in fear of the fire.

Yet, like you, I am also a child of Abraham and Isaac. And I try to live by the Ten Commandments given on high unto Moses.

And, also, I suspect like you I have been influenced by the traditional knowledge and faith of the original peoples of our coast, especially concerning the relationship between human beings and our brothers and sisters in the animal kingdom.

You are such a unique figure in British Columbian society that I salute you and pledge myself to endeavour in a small way to follow your example and teachings.

Thank you for the great kindness and honour that you have shown to our family.

Yours respectfully with love,
Michael (sent from London)

At the time I was preparing to undertake a long-anticipated, four-month circumnavigation of the world. I decided it might be preferable to reply when I was literally and figuratively at sea. By the time "the spirit moved me," it was seven months later. With his generous permission, Michael has since consented to my request to share this private correspondence.

***Reply***
*May 2019*
*The Atlantic Ocean*
*Latitude: 33° 03.63' N*
*Longitude: 052° 39.64' W*

Dear Michael, I received the clarion email that you sent me as you flew across the Atlantic en route to Jerusalem the Golden (*Yerushalayim shel Zahav*). Protocol and good manners dictated that I should have responded in kind a few days later but here was my dilemma: what you wrote pierced me so deeply that I could only read a few sentences a day. Even after completing the reading I was overwhelmed and felt unworthy of your sentiments. I left my response for another week and then another, and finally a promise to write by Christmas. None of those materialized. Soon after, I embarked on a four-month world cruise and thought to write you from some inspiring part of the globe.

It is only now—also in the midst of the Atlantic, in the waving waters half way between Ireland and Florida—that these words can tumble forth. I'm not sure what I'll write but this I do know: these words belong to you. I will express myself soul-to-soul, primitive psyche one to another, pilgrim-to-pilgrim upon a planet's unwritten but always revealing path. Forgive me if I now use you as a screen for my own projections. Read what I offer in a few minutes or wait a year, or ignore it altogether. This is written for you, *A Letter to Michael*, to be scattered upon the God-given winds.

My intentions are not to praise or adulate you: that would not only be inappropriate but also make you uncomfortable and embarrassed. These words serve as a personal witness to your honest, lonely, noble struggles to know yourself and to act accordingly. My words are a gift to you just as yours were a present to me.

There are things that humble souls dare not speak, even whisper, to themselves let alone to others. So the Lord created friends and witnesses so that we might be seen if only "through a dim mirror."[105] That you should refer to me as Brother Yosef . . . That was enough for tears to flow and heart to break. I am in your debt. I will always act towards you as a supportive brother, a mendicant at your call.

I'm glad that "A Sleep of Prisoners" became a poetical prayer mantra on your polar flight to London. I continue to be intrigued by your varied family history extending through numerous locations in Europe, North America and now Asia. I trust that someday you will write your autobiography (or work with someone to help produce an authorized biography).[106]

I find that those closest to us, such as family, might not be inclined to read such a tome. It is too close to home. They know us in another way, as the Bible reminds us: "There is no prophet in his own home" (*Luke* 4:24; *Mark* 6:4). In any event, such a volume—even if it can only touch on the headlines and introduce a number of topics—is of value to the writer as a catharsis and to the community for its historic and inspirational narrative.

I am so gratified that you enjoyed reading my convocation addresses. Just as I may be one of the few who could write about spirituality, religion and art, so you are one of the few who could fully understand and appreciate it. I'm sure that if we—perhaps with a few others—entered into conversation on the topic we could amplify the ideas and references considerably. As for the gifts wrapped in the Blue Shawl: they were carefully curated, things that I thought might enhance your pilgrimage both before, during and after the travels.

And now to comment on a few other subjects as suggested by your email:

### *Humility*

You write that you "feel so unworthy of [my] kindness and attention." I understand and yet it is I who tremble to present these metaphorical gifts to you and Yoshi. I do not want to seem invasive of your privacy, time or space, yet I feel that what I share with you is as a friend, a fellow pilgrim on the path. We are both aware of the biblical obligation to return that which is lost to its rightful owner.[107] Likewise, if I see something that "belongs" to you, I take it as my honour and duty to make sure you receive it. But I do it with respect and will never take advantage of your precious sense of solitude.

Eliot, in a poem that I've included at the end of this letter, wrote that "The only wisdom we can hope to acquire is the wisdom of humility."

When speaking about humility the bible reminds us: "Now the man Moses was very humble, more than anyone upon the face of the earth" (*Num.* 12:3). We often mistake the term "humble" for someone who is reticent to participate fully in life and community. And yet the humble accomplish great things. The surprising axiom is that the more truly humble the person is, the deeper he can see and the higher he can soar. *False* humility is a weakness filled with fear and reluctance. *True* humility, however, is a strength wherein one knows one's time and place, one's opportunities and responsibilities. False humility is afraid of its shadow; true humility will wrestle with darkness, chaos and confusion for the sake of light, love, and justice.

Moses may have been humble—a reluctant prophet, an outsider, a child sentenced to death at birth, a Prince of Egypt who exiled himself to the desert, someone who spoke better with goats than with people—yet it was precisely *he* who was chosen to act as God's ambassador. He organized an entire nation (negotiating with his own unknown people, including its rebels), spoke face to face with the Divine and with pharaoh (with kings and the King of kings), led millions to freedom and transmitted a heavenly mandate that has persisted until our day. It was precisely because he emptied his ego so completely that the Creator was able to fill him with visions and directives never afforded another human being.

The *midrash* recognized how God often spoke through the humble: The reluctant prophet rather than the arrogant leader,[108] the Burning Bush rather than an imposing Oak, and choosing Mount Sinai as the location for the giving of Divine Revelation as opposed to presenting it on a more prominent elevation.

In the midst of your innate humility you, too, continue to be lauded for your accomplishments.

Congratulations on being recognized by *Vancouver Magazine* as one of the highest-ranking Power 50 in the province. The magazine wrote: "Michael Audain continues to reign as a benevolent Renaissance prince of Vancouver, a gracious man who … ."

These words, which effectively coronate you as the proverbial Philosopher King, could only have been written by others who recognized you by your labour, by the fruit that grew from your good tree.[109]

When it comes to your humility, I also remember your reluctant yet noble movement through the Eagle Dance at the Whistler dedication of the Dance Screen.[110] There you were—tall, thin, extended arms-become-wings, bedecked in shamanic robes and concealed behind headband and avian mask, befeathered, you danced with the artist, the chief. With the screen behind, the music around and you within, the gallery was transformed into the vast reaches of eagles' realms, the heart of heaven, the mountain nests on high. All those present—appreciative for all that you had done for them and for others—were wishing you well. It was a rare moment for there was not a jealous eye in the house. All were filled with gratitude to be part of such a transcendent experience.

As for those who use false humility as an excuse *not* to get involved, here are three fine quotes:

> "A ship in harbour is safe, but that is not what ships are built for." — *John Augustus Shedd*

> "Every man is guilty of all the good he did not do." — *Voltaire*

> "Have courage for the great sorrows of life and patience for the small ones; and when you have laboriously accomplished your daily task, go to sleep in peace." — *Victor Hugo*[111]

For a humorous quote illustrating the flip side of humility: William Patrick "W. P." Kinsella, OC OBC (May 25, 1935–September 16,

2016) often quoted Hilaire Belloc who wrote, "When I am dead, I hope it may be said: 'His sins were scarlet, but his books were read.'"

### Sin and transgression

In your note you wrote that:

> *I am really just a poor sinner who is making this trip in the hope that praying in the very places where Christ Jesus was born, lived, taught and died will somewhat help me repent so that my many sins may be washed clean.*

I admire your sense of self and sin. Your pilgrimage to the Holy Land and then to *Urbs Sacra* upon the Seven Roman Hills for a blessing from *il Papa*, fulfills theological, emotional, physical and intellectual dimensions. Reading your reflections about being a sinner initiated a number of personal reflections.

The idea and practice of repentance is both powerful and necessary. It indicates your sensitivity to others, to God, to your own soul, as well as to all of creation. You are indeed a unique individual in our community, composed of a combination of innate shyness and universal awareness. Through the lens of your gentle nature you were gifted with great empathy for others.

But you were not satisfied only with *feelings*. You also turned those emotions into practical *actions*. With the gift of your exceptional intellect you studied at the highest levels; you travelled in order to learn from others in a series of unmitigated experiences; you spoke out; organized social justice for the disadvantaged and for those who were silenced; you observed the country and wrote policy for the government; built homes for those without shelter and for the dreamers; you made a fair profit, spent wisely, and then generously shared with millions of others. You also became a champion for the natural environment—in the forests and oceans—and felt your soul emanate in the guise of the Grizzly and Spirit Bears as well as migrating salmon. Similar to the Creator whose first labours were as a builder and artist, you collected art that moved you, encouraged others to create "in the Image of God," and then you helped to support and build temple-type galleries, filling them with aesthetic treasures, archetypes of the national soul.

And still you repent. How could such an active man *not* sin; how could such an explorer into so many kingdoms *not* get lost once in a while? It is precisely because of your self-awareness that you repent, that you clear the path, ask forgiveness and pray to stand pure and blameless before the Anointed One of all Eternity, before your own personal deity, the Friend, the Origin, Source, Alpha and Omega.

I am reminded of the Confessions of Augustine . . .

When I was in Belfast a couple of weeks ago I hired a driver/guide to show me the sights. Besides visiting the Titanic Museum, gardens and other museums, spending time discussing The Troubles and seeing various parts of the curfew gates and painted walls, I asked him to take us to Downpatrick where there is an interpretive centre on the life of Saint Patrick, a cathedral on the hill and one of many purported burial sites of the Irish saint, the Apostle of Ireland. This, too, was a kind of sacred journey. At Downpatrick I learned about the life of an extraordinary man and was introduced to his letters that are now considered to be the beginning of Irish written literature. The two most important letters were his *Letter to the Soldiers of Coroticus* and his *Confessio*.

In his *Letter to the Soldiers of Coroticus* he wrote as you might have:

> I declare that I, Patrick, an unlearned sinner indeed, have been established a bishop in Ireland. I hold quite certainly that what I am, I have accepted from God.
>
> And Scripture also says: "What does it profit a person to gain the whole world and yet suffer the loss of his or her soul?"

And in *St Patrick's Confession*, circa 460–490 C.E., he penned:

> *Ego Patricius, peccator rusticissimus et minimus omnium fidelium et contemptibilis sum apud plurimos* ... My name is Patrick. I am a sinner, a simple country person, and the least of all believers. I am looked down upon by many ... .
>
> So I am first of all a simple country person, a refugee, and unlearned. I do not know how to provide for the future. But this I know for certain, that before I was brought low, I was like a stone lying deep in the mud. Then he who is powerful came and in his mercy pulled me out, and lifted me up and placed me on the very top of the wall. That is why I must shout aloud in return to the Lord for such great good deeds of his, here and now and forever, which the human mind cannot measure.

Dear Michael, in spite of the great achievements that you have accomplished and the numerous laurels bestowed upon your gracious brow, I can only imagine how you must have struggled within. As a fellow pilgrim (our paths may have been different but our ultimate goals similar), I, with others on the way, can appreciate the "long and winding road." So much had to be concealed. Who could we trust? Who might betray our confidence? How much is private, what do we dare share to unburden ourselves, and with whom?—A friend, a lover, in drunken stupor, in confessional repentance, to a therapist, a stranger ... ? How many times did we have to begin again vowing never to repeat those varied transgressions and often one principal addiction that drew us back upon its temporary power, its transient thrill.

For men—at least this has been my personal experience—these "transgressions" or "psychological actings out" are often related to sexual and power issues (*Eros*) or to abandonment and survival

(*Thanatos*). Yes, there *is* legitimate guilt and transgression in many of our actions for which we are responsible, *but* for so many others perhaps grace and forgiveness—from the Creator who made us like this—is more becoming. What I am implying is that the Holy One is also somewhat implicated in our transgressions.

How many times did we have to admit to our failures and weaknesses? And how many times did we struggle to the point of exhaustion? I think of your athletic background as a pugilist, as the metaphorical boxer who, like Jacob, wrestled with the angel disguised as a man—the angel of his twin brother; his shadow angel; the angel that attempted to block him from his return to family, country and destiny; the angel who feigned welcome but portended death. It was that same night angel who, as dawn approached, renamed him Israel, *Godwrestler*: "Your name will no longer be Jacob, but Israel [*Yisrael*], because you have struggled with God and with people, and you have prevailed" (*Gen.* 32).

Like Jacob you have become an Israel. You can say along with Timothy (*2 Tim.* 4:7), "I have fought the good fight; I have finished my course; I have kept the faith."

Meanwhile, you have lived an exemplary life in spite of what you consider a long litany of transgressions. This, too, is the "way of the world," as the wise Solomon intoned, "Surely there is not a righteous one on earth who does [only] good and never sins."[112]

To conclude these reflections on transgression and struggle, below are some thoughts I wrote last summer as part of an email correspondence with a friend about the nature of Grace and Sin in Jewish thought. These are preliminary considerations.

## Email Correspondence re. Sin, Grace, Repentance

**From**: Douglas Todd
**Subject: Sin boldly etc.**
**Date**: July 27, 2018
**To**: Yosef Wosk

Hello Yosef,
Hope all is well in the heat.

I have a theological kind of question.

What is the Hebrew tradition's way of talking about grace?

I'm thinking of Luther's famous quote, "Sin boldly, so grace may abound."

(I know Luther may not be the greatest person to bring up, given his antisemitism, but ...)

I'm thinking about believing in grace (undeserved love), etc. as the antidote to having excessive guilt for one's own wrongdoing, major and minor.

For instance, I pretty well think we're sinning all the time, even in ways we don't know. We're constantly hurting people and being imperfect and, systemically, holding great power that others don't have. And I'm thinking about theological ways to overcome possible guilt one could feel about constantly being imperfect, to say the least.

A person could have tremendous moral scrupulosity that makes it impossible for them to let even the simplest possible transgression go. Can this be considered within the norms of religious righteousness or is it a disorder of some sort? I am wondering if you could provide some Jewish wisdom regarding letting go of such guilt.

Any thoughts or phrases, famous and otherwise, from Hebrew tradition?

Thanks for thinking about this.
Doug

**From**: Yosef Wosk
**Subject: Re: Sin boldly etc.**
**Date**: August 1, 2018
**To**: Douglas Todd

Dear Doug,

The last few days I've been feeling kind of burned out and moving slowly in the midst of Summer. It is a combination of having so much to do and not enough time in which to do it, but also a gentle letting go of incessantly commenting on situations, of getting involved and changing, building or cleaning up. Sometimes I just STOP and accept things the way they are.

What a relief; what a love affair—temporary as it is—with reality. I will, however, attempt a response.

I'm not an expert on Grace in various Jewish schools of thought through the ages. For diversified articles—and a wide variety of opinions—search the Net for "Grace in Judaism".

There is nothing in mainstream Judaism that I know of that coincides with Luther's quote. There have been a few wayward heretical mystics, however, who have come close to it. For an example, search the Net for "Jacob Frank Jewish mystical heretic".

Folk wisdom, filled with cathartic humour on the subject of engaging in an irresistible transgression, is exemplified in a saying of my friend's grandfather: "If you're going to eat *treif* (non-kosher meat), eat it until the fat drips from your lips." That is, if you're going to involve yourself surreptitiously in a sin, then do it fully, completely and with enjoyment. Do it and get it over with. There is always room for atonement. This statement does not even mention the idea of grace but I suppose it assumes forgiveness along with later repentance.

If you're thinking about welcoming grace as an antidote to excessive guilt, then I'd say embrace it now and then continue to investigate it over the next couple of years. Jewish tradition is filled not just with admonitions of borders, boundaries and judgment [*din, gevurah, mishpat*] but also with overflowing loving kindness, forgiveness, understanding and grace [*hain, hesed, rahamim*].

Re. sinning all the time: Search Net for "King David My sin is always before me." This quote is from *Psalm* 51:3; also see *Psalm* 32:5. Although David may be referring to one or two particular transgressions you bring up a most sensitive concept—that we are sinning all the time.

Jean Paul Sartre discussed something similar in his secular concept of Existentialism, i.e. that we are all guilty simply because we were born, because we exist. Human beings live in constant anguish, he wrote, simply because we are condemned to be free. Abraham Joshua Heschel referred to this as "the insecurity of freedom." Sartre's point, however, is a secular concept, not connected to Christianity's Original Sin.

I recently had a discussion with Max Wyman wherein he advised me to prioritize my labours, not to get bogged down in too many superficial or extraneous projects or obligations and, instead, to focus on the major important ones. I thanked him but then said that I still feel guilty about not doing all the other menial tasks and that I felt some responsibility for others. He countered that in my and his religions, guilt plays a major role but that it must be ignored, seen as a hindrance or illusion in all but the most egregious actions (I am paraphrasing).

Your sensitivity is commendable and in some respects I agree with you: We are sinning all the time—whether consciously or unconsciously, with intent or by mistake. We are constantly hurting or disappointing others and busy being imperfect. These actions/attributes, however, only describe part of the picture, for we are also just as busy admiring and loving others, assisting them and striving for perfection. All this is part of the human condition, the polarities of being. We are sometimes elegant in our speech, brilliant in our thought and superbly athletic in our movement. Conversely, at other times we misspeak, break hearts and manipulate others, just as we are foolish and clumsy beings. We cheer for winners but condemn others often. Damn it, we are all in need of grace regardless of our beliefs or lack thereof.

More to discuss re. what you wrote "about theological ways to overcome possible guilt one could feel about constantly being imperfect."

On the one hand, guilt serves as a kind of creative tension that constantly leads one to accomplish something in an effort to assuage the guilt. On the other hand, unbridled guilt could soon prove debilitating, too much of a constant burden to bear.

Look at p. 22 (and the related endnotes) in the book I gave you (Five Blessings and a Dare). There is a discussion re. our two pockets. In one pocket is the attitude of grace and gratitude, of "The world was created just for me"; in the other pocket is the attitude of despair, of constant transgression, of "I am nothing but dust and ashes." We need them both in order to live with a combination of gratitude and humility, seeking to strike a balance between the extremes of arrogant self-identity and denigrating nihilism. It is only when the humility—or, conversely, the mania of goodness or fanatical championing any ideal—becomes excessive or pathological that it becomes a problem.

So be aware of your potential transgressions. Don't commit them on purpose unless you must. As Oscar Wilde famously observed: "I can resist everything except temptation."

Then, in recovery, consider your indiscretions and return to ask forgiveness from the other, the Spirit, and yourself. The Hebrew word for repentance is *tshuvah*, which means to return, to answer, to respond.

Let Grace be your Lady, Spirit Incarnate. Let her embrace you, and you her, when healing consolation is required or when you want to enter into deep wordless dialogue with Love, Favour and Kindness. You will emerge with a light-filled visage and a profound sense of well-being.

Looking at myself and considering you, I feel there is also grist for the therapeutic mill here.

Besides theological beliefs, what drives us to feel that we're sinning all the time, hurting others, abusing our powers? The human brain is an exquisite instrument. Like any other technology, however, it is prone to glitches, malfunctions. If one suspects a disorder, follow it to its source. Our minds communicate through stories but often there are conflicting versions, not all of which have happy endings. Don't let any belief system become an excuse for insanity or its many tributaries. Don't allow psychological disturbances, however well-intentioned, to masquerade as balanced righteousness.

I'm so glad that you've brought up this topic because through your published words you do hold significant power.

As *Proverbs* 18:21 says: "Life and death are in the power of the tongue, and those who love it will eat its fruits." Meaning, those who abuse talk (or any communications) will suffer its inevitable consequences; those who respect it will, in turn, be admired. This sentiment is repeated many times in Scripture including: "For by your words you will be acquitted, and by your words you will be condemned" (*Matthew* 12:37), and "The words of a wise one's mouth are gracious, but the lips of a fool will consume him" (*Eccles.* 10:12–14).

Also see *www.gotquestions.org/power-of-the-tongue.html*. Tongue = words, however expressed. According to the Book of Genesis, the world was created through words; it can also be destroyed in the same way. And, of course, the dramatic opening from the Gospel of John: "In the beginning was the Word, and the Word was with God, and the Word was God."

May your eyes continue to open, your heart to heal, your mind to observe and comment. As long as your attitude is positive, your intentions pure and your doubts offer a stabilizing internal commentary, then you will be fine.

May you be blessed with inspiration to share in the ongoing task of the daily creation of heaven and earth.

Your friend and fellow traveller on Starship Gaia,
Yosef

### Indigenous Arts

Michael, in your email you wrote:

> And, also, I suspect like you I have been influenced by the traditional knowledge and faith of the original peoples of our coast, especially concerning the relationship between human beings and our brothers and sisters in the animal kingdom.

It is obvious that you have been at the forefront of collecting, organizing, exhibiting and providing for research for the Indigenous Arts not only in British Columbia but also across the country. We all have so much for which to thank you. You have also inspired me to initiate a major project, one that perhaps I should have told you about last year, or even asked your permission first.

After two years of conversation with Jim Hart—casual at first but then serious—I have commissioned him, and he has accepted, to create a monumental carving that will take about three years to complete. After finding the appropriate trees, he began a few months ago to carve on Haida Gwaii what will be a historically unique piece: a hybrid Haida-Hebrew large curved screen. It will incorporate a complimentary set of iconographies derived from both traditions.

Each Hebrew tribe will be represented by their biblical totems depicted in the blessings of Jacob and Moses; there are numerous biblical and rabbinic references to animals; besides the Haida eagle and raven, the dove will also be carved; Moses will be the shaman;

the three forefathers and four grandmothers will be depicted; salmon and the bear will be present alongside Behemoth and the Leviathan, etc. We spent a year of on-and-off conversation and then Jim began to prepare the design sketch.

I had been imagining some such carving for about twenty-five years. At first, I thought it might be two large totem poles, each pole depicting six of the original twelve biblical tribes. I considered asking Robert Davidson to carve it but in three encounters with him scattered over a number of years, I didn't feel a natural connection. I've known Jim for about twenty years but it wasn't until I really stopped to consider all the elements—including my getting older and having to make time-bound decisions—that I decided to approach him about this commission.

The magnificent dance screen that Jim and his assistants carved for the Audain Art Museum was the final inspiration. I have also engaged talented individuals, including some associated with MOA,[113] to follow the progress, write a book on the piece, produce a short film and develop related public programming when the time comes. The final large concave curved screen—about 14' high and 18' long—will be installed outdoors in our home garden. I still shudder at the thought of having actually done this. Your tacit influence was essential.

### Poetry Offerings

But first this quote about teachers found in a friendly anarchist bookstore that I stumbled upon in Amsterdam last month:

> "The task of teachers, those obscure soldiers of civilization,
>    is to give people the intellectual means to revolt."

I love those words describing teachers as *those obscure soldiers of civilization*. The quote is from Louise Michel (1830–1905), a French anarchist, school teacher and medical worker who wrote these sentiments in her *Memories of 1886*.

I didn't realize that you had such a profound appreciation for poetry, in this case Fry's "A Sleep of Prisoners." You wrote: "I read this prayer from 'A Sleep of Prisoners' over and over in the early dawn until it became part of me."

Yours is not just a cursory appreciation or a guarded and distant intellectual understanding but rather a wholehearted numinous involvement in the experience. You don't just read poetry, you become the poem. That is how I've felt in our garden the past few years. *The poetry of garden* where each letter is a leaf, every image a flower, all plants a Tree of Life, a metaphysical flight of forever.

Two poems offered today. The first is by the Israeli poet Zelda Mishkovsky (1914–1984) and the second by Eliot.

### *Each Man Has A Name*

Each man has a name, given him by God, and given him by
    his father and mother.
Each man has a name given him by his stature and his way
    of smiling,
and given him by his clothes.
Each man has a name given him by the mountains and
    given him by his walls.
Each man has a name given him by the planets and given
    him by his neighbours.
Each man has a name given him by his sins and given him
    by his longing.
Each man has a name given him by his enemies and given
    him by his love.
Each man has a name given him by his feast days and given
    him by his craft.

> Each man has a name given him by the seasons and given
>     him by his blindness.
> Each man has a name given him by the sea and given him by
>     his death.¹¹⁴

The last is a poem with which I am sure you are familiar. T. S. Eliot, "East Coker," Number 2 from *The Four Quartets*. There is so much here that I feel would resonate with you but I'll restrain myself to quoting just a few lines.¹¹⁵

> Old men ought to be explorers
> Here or there does not matter
> We must be still and still moving
> Into another intensity
> For a further union, a deeper communion
> Through the dark cold and the empty desolation,
> The wave cry, the wind cry, the vast waters
> Of the petrel and the porpoise. In my end is my beginning.

### Conclusion

In the end, yes, we are all the children of Abraham and Sarah, Isaac and Rebecca, Jacob with Leah and Rahel. The children of stars and primeval seas, compassionate buddhas, beggars, priests, seekers and saints. We are also the progeny of rogues and rascals, of those who were ill in body or cursed with afflicted minds, and descendants of just plain folk who were thankful to survive yet another difficult day.

You and I, along with everyone else, are fellow passengers on a precious planet; we are wounded warriors for justice and witness to creation as it fills the universe. But most of all we are allies and friends created in the Image of God. We are also a bridge between the Creator and His creation, for we are the world made aware of itself. Our being here is not a passive planting: we have also been instructed to cultivate and protect this garden globe.[116]

After four months at sea we complete our circumnavigation in two days. I am filled with gratitude for having participated in the journey. I look forward to returning home safely along with tens of books, dozens of gifts, a hundred mementos, ten thousand digital photographs, tea and spices from the Far East, fragrant incense from Sri Lanka and the desert sands of Petra, a carving of the Komodo Dragon, memories of new friends and fifty expeditions, having transited both canals and entered ancient kingdoms both lost and found, having written essays and emails, and turning seventy in the warm womb of the Indian Ocean.

Michael, thank you for receiving these words of reflection. There is enough here so I won't disturb you again for a year. Unless I find just the right book for your library. Also, please don't feel obligated in any way to respond to these musings; I know you are already busy enough. If there is anything I can do for you, please let me know. I would be happy to assist in any way you deem appropriate.

All the very best to Yoshi.

Yosef, with 16,874 feet of water under our keel and two sleeps 'til landfall

# T. S. Eliot
# Four Quartets

*The Teacher stands near the edge, daring the student to fly.* From a circa 1475 illustration of Hermes Trismegistus bedecked in Arabic dress with turban and royal crown; in the alchemistical manuscript Florence, Biblioteca Medicea Laurenziana, Ashb. 1166, fol. 1v. Heading: *Pater Hermes philosophorum* (Hermes, father of the philosophers).

# FIVE BLESSINGS AND A DARE: AUDACIOUS ADVICE FOR STUDENTS

*This article is based upon Y.W.'s message to graduating students when he received an honorary doctor of letters from Simon Fraser University on June 14, 2012. A fuller version, with a Preface by Douglas Todd that originally appeared in the Vancouver Sun, was produced as a limited edition, marbled paper hardcover chapbook by Aryel Publishing House in 2018. — Ed.*

I am going to speak about what I have learned, presented as some hard-earned advice in the guise of five surprising blessings and a dare. I will give only headlines, speak in exaggerated terms, enthuse you to live your life with a kind of soulful brilliance and trust that "a hint is sufficient for the wise."

### The Five Blessings

Today I advocate that you all become Beggars, Thieves, Fools, Arrogant and Masters of Destruction. I realize that these may be rather shocking offerings but here they are.

## 1. Beggars

Beggars are not just the poor and downtrodden but also holy beggars, those who realize how inconsequential they really are compared to the fullness of the universe. They may be professional beggars who claim a street corner or itinerant mendicants who wander the world with purpose (it must be remembered that not all who wander are lost). Constantly humbled and mired in the vicissitudes of an uncertain future, they experience the essential nature of life.[117]

But they, too, are continually giving. I've learned from beggars that we are one another in disguise. They've taught me how to ask[118] and how to receive,[119] and how to beg for knowledge, love and life because there are so many things that we just cannot accomplish alone.

It is those modest ones that I refer to when I wish we could all become like them and share a meal at the Beggars Banquet to come.

## 2. Thieves

I trust that this graduating class will be among the most honest and ethical, and yet to truly succeed in your studies you must also learn from thieves who are always looking to profit from what is not yet theirs.[120]

This applies, of course, only to learning. It is categorized as *kinat sofrim*, "jealousy of the scholars,"[121] for when you see someone of greater learning or accomplishment you may desire to be like them.[122]

Not everything can be transmitted from teacher to student: Some things must be seized by the student alone.[123] Listen how the Taoist teacher, Sat Hon, explains it.

> I tell my students the best mode of learning is to pretend you are a thief. If you come with a sense of entitlement because you've paid for the lesson, you will be passive. You can wait for ten years and say, "How come you didn't show me that?" and I can say, "I *have* been showing it to you but you haven't been skillful enough to steal it from me."[124]

## 3. *Fools*

I wish that you become not only domesticated and highly trained scholars but that you also embrace the Crazy Wisdom[125] of those who live life large, those who are intoxicated with ideas and eager to see them realized.

To accomplish this you sometimes need to play the fool, to stand on your head,[126] to see things upside down and sideways,[127] inside out and from a distance.[128] If you are fortunate, you may slip into a state of mystical union where the knower, the knowledge and the known are one.

Being a fool is when you can devote yourself wholeheartedly to achieving a worthwhile goal. You are *meshugah le'davar ehad*, "crazy for one thing."[129]

Yet the Fool does not just live a life defined by obsessive hard-edged results. His path is paved with poetry and rung by resonant bells; her story is garbed in spontaneity, filled with humour and electrified by an infinity of alternatives.

## 4. *Arrogant*

The fourth blessing is that you proclaim your arrogance, not just your humility. Everyone has two pockets: One carries the egotistical attitude of me and mine, of "the world was created just for me." The other pocket balances the first. It carries the attitude of insignificance, of "I am but dust and ashes."[130]

There are times when the first pocket, that of supreme confidence, even arrogance, is called for. It is an intense experience often accompanied by an attitude of joyous self-reliance that can strengthen your thoughts and transform your visions.

It can also save your life as it did Buckminster Fuller's[131] when he was a young man and depressed by a series of disappointments.[132] A second before suicide he heard a voice urging him instead to embark on "an experiment to find what a single individual can contribute to changing the world and benefiting all humanity."[133]

That humble man was saved by an outburst of arrogance and became one of the most original thinkers of the past one hundred years. May confidence be your ally and a reminder that you are exceptional and a type of genius in your own right; that you have a gift like no other[134] to benefit the world.

If you still insist on belittling yourself, hiding in the pocket of distorted humility,[135] then listen to this ancient story of just how much the Life Force encourages our growth:

> Over every blade of grass
> an angel hovers
> with a stick in its hand.
> As it strikes the plant
> it calls out —
> "Grow! Grow!"[136]

### 5. *Masters of Destruction*

This last blessing is that you become iconoclasts, breakers of false beliefs and destroyers of delusions.

I'm not referring to violent destruction but rather to *creative destruction* that clears the way for renewal.[137] I'm alluding to surrendering negative personal beliefs and dispelling fatalistic fantasies that impose their unconscious tyranny over our lives. Our days may be passed in sleepwalking and our years in yearning but never doing. I have learned that to fulfill my dreams I must wake up. All birth requires prior destruction: The waters that break, the seed that sprouts, the earth that parts, the shell that shatters.

Entire civilizations sometimes need to be defied.[138] My teacher, Ha'Rav Dovid Lifshitz, once stopped our class and challenged us: "You students," he said, "are too impressed with the idea of civilization.[139] During the last war, who was the most civilized of all nations? The Nazis emerged from a culture of composers and philosophers, of authors and scientists, and yet what did they do?

With one hand they played the piano and with the other they strangled children."

That is why I encourage you to become great builders when you can but dauntless destroyers when necessary.

The most difficult subjects are ourselves. The illusions are more complex for they insulate our sanity. But if we don't banish those self-deceptions we will remain prisoners barricaded within the confines of our own minds.

Over the years I have been fortunate to find teachers who urged me to fling open the Gates of Perception[140] and not to wait for Kafka's doorkeeper to declare "No one else could ever be admitted here since this gate was meant only for you. I am now going to shut it."[141]

Even if ten thousand obstacles stand in your way, you can summon ten thousand-and-one strategies to overcome them. That is how you will arrive at your destination[142] transformed by your efforts as a Master of Creative Destruction.

### *The Unyielding Journey*

Today you are what might be designated as UAOs, "Unidentified Academic Objects."[143] Tomorrow you will pursue your future and consolidate your reputations. Life often feels like a series of déjà vu phenomena where completing one level only puts you in the kindergarten of what is still to come.

The path is long and the journey unyielding.[144] I spent most of my life being lost, climbing, searching, falling, finding and struggling to arise.

I discovered that brains can be awakened no matter our age, and hearts, however closed, can be reinvented; that arms, even if passive, can now reach out; and that souls, even if wounded, can soar, unbound, once again.

## Conclusion

I urged you to be brazen thieves and holy beggars, inverted fools and arrogant masters of destruction. May you be further incited to live your lives with the passion of lovers and the stamina of athletes to achieve your goals "with all your heart, with all your soul and with all your might."[145]

And finally, *the dare.* I conclude with a compelling parable attributed to Apollinaire[146] in which we overhear a dramatic discussion between a teacher and students. Not just a teacher of facts and fictions but a teacher of life. I have learned that there is no corner of the cosmos where wisdom does not dwell. Guides are everywhere—in the winds and waves, fires and fields.[147] Listen and they will speak,[148] daring us to come ever closer to where we need to be.

> *"Come to the edge,"* he said.
> *"We are afraid,"* they said.
> *"Come to the edge,"* he said.
> They came.
> He pushed them.
> And they flew.

# NASREDDIN

All the villagers had gathered in their 13th-century mosque to hear the famously wise teacher Nasreddin.

"Do you know what I'm going to speak about today?" he asked.

"No, no, of course we don't!" answered the stunned villagers.

"Well, then," Nasreddin replied as he left the building, "I refuse to waste my time on a bunch of ignoramuses like you."

The next day he was invited back. Once again he asked. "Who knows what I'm going to speak about today?"

This time, afraid that he would leave, they called out: "I do; we do!"

To which he replied, "If you already know, then I don't need to waste my time repeating it."

And he left the building.

Even though the people were perplexed they still wanted to hear the teacher's wisdom and so they invited him back a third time.

"Who knows what I'm going to speak about today?" he asked.

This time they had a plan. Half answered, "I do, we do," and the other half responded, "No, no, we don't."

To which he replied, "Good! Then let those who know tell those who don't."

And with that, he left for the last time.

*A bronze sculpture of Nasreddin in Bukhara, Uzbekistan.*

# THREE POEMS FROM HAIDA GWAII

*Masset moment*

Did I just catch a glimpse of you
or was that an iridescent humming bird
standing still on the air
of its imagined desire?

*Spray*

The healing fragrance
of salty sea air,
reminiscent of spilt semen
gently impregnating
yet another promising day

### Iron & stone

Sacrificial altars
in the ancient world
were left rough-hewn.

Bringing an iron chisel
upon the natural
spirit-dwelling stone
would drive out the daemon
and render the rock impotent.
Iron, an instrument of war,
was not to be introduced
to the votive shrine,
mediating table of peace.

# ENDNOTES

1   There are a series of online articles outlining biblical references including "Biblical Number #420 in the Bible—Meaning and Symbolism." For an article linking "angel numbers and Tarot cards" see the online article "Do you know there is a connection between angel numbers and Tarot cards? Here's how angel number 420 is connected" by Soumi Pyne in Hindustan Times, November 18, 2023. An article on biblical numerology is "The Biblical Meaning of 420" by Aurelia, July 20, 2024; and for the cannabis culture connection see "Here's the Real Reason we Associate 420 with Weed" by Olivia Waxman, on Time.com, updated April 8, 2024.

2   *Steppenwolf,* Hermann Hesse, translated from German; 1st edition, Henry Holt Publishing, New York, 1929.

3   Cf. "The collision: Fred Herzog, the Holocaust and me," by Marsha Lederman, *The Globe and Mail,* May 5, 2012.

4   Cf. *Wikipedia* article "Filius philosophorum," and "The Alchemical Symbolism of the Lapis Philosophorum" on the *Esoteric Avenue* website.

5   A song by the Eagles released on February 22, 1977, a month before our trip to the USSR.

6   Those nostalgic cardboard-backed thin plastic writing pads that we had not used since we were children. You can write your message or draw a picture on the surface and then erase it by lifting the top thin transparent plastic overlay.

7   "Evil Empire" was used in a speech by President Ronald Reagan on March 8, 1983 to refer to the Soviet Union at the height of the Cold War.

8   Cf. Online Quote Investigator—"Who Ya Gonna Believe, Me or Your Own Eyes?"

9   "The Red Army was the main engine of Nazism's destruction," writes British historian and journalist Max Hastings in *Inferno: The World at War, 1939-1945*. "The Soviet Union paid the harshest price: though the numbers are not exact, an estimated 26 million Soviet citizens died during World War II, including as many as 11 million soldiers. At the same time, the Germans suffered three-quarters of their wartime losses fighting the Red Army." [Excerpt from article "Don't forget how the Soviet Union saved the world from Hitler," by Ishaan Tharoor, *The Washington Post*, May 8, 2015].

10   "In Soviet Ukraine [where my father was born], Soviet Belarus [where my mother was born when it was still in eastern Poland], and the Leningrad district, lands where the Stalinist regime had starved and shot some four million people in the previous eight years, German forces managed to starve and shoot even more in half the time," historian Timothy Snyder writes in *Bloodlands: Europe between Hitler and Stalin*. [Note: Content in square brackets added by this author.] He reports that between 1933 and 1945 in the "bloodlands"—the broad sweep of territory on the periphery of the Soviet and Nazi realms—some 14 million civilians were killed.

11   Sharansky eventually spent nine years in Soviet prisons. As the result of an international campaign he was released on February 11, 1986 and immigrated to Israel where he continued with his participation in politics and human rights. His book *Fear No Evil* (1988) is a memoir of the Jewish refuseniks, his show trial on charges of espionage, incarceration by the KGB and liberation. When Elie Wiesel died in 2016, Sharansky—who became the face of the Soviet Jewish struggle, and his wife, Avital, who with Wiesel and others led advocacy for Sharansky's release from prison—commented: "Elie Wiesel was the collective moral compass of the Jewish people. He was the first to break the silence surrounding the plight of Soviet Jewry, and he accompanied our struggle until we achieved victory." Wiesel's 1966 book reporting on the plight of Soviet Jewry, *The Jews of Silence*, helped awaken the movement that sought their freedom.

12   Online article on The Culture Factor website, *Ask An Expert: Smile In Russia* by Pia Kahara. It is worthwhile reading this fascinating article that describes significant cultural implications of the smile.

13   I remember a subsequent visit to Cuba during Fidel Castro's time in office. We met a number of individuals who were careful what they said but not afraid to speak with us. One man, a doctor, asked if we had any connections in Canada or the United States where he might find a job. His salary for being a psychologist and doctor in Havana was $24 a month. In the workers' paradise of Communist Cuba the government considered that sufficient as all other basic expenses were taken care of by the state.

14   BBC website "Managing the Cold War 1962–1985: Danger of Mutually Assured Destruction."

15   Based on Robert Browning's poem *Andrea del Sarto* which reads: "Ah, but a man's reach should exceed his grasp, / Or what's a heaven for?" Jean Houston

cleverly rephrased it as: "A man's reach should exceed his grasp or what's a meta for [metaphor]?"

16   *Genesis* 1:4, 10, 12, 18, 21, 31.

17   Many of these thoughts have been influenced by *kabbalah,* Jewish mysticism, as well as by Ralph Waldo Emerson's essay "Art" (*Emerson's Works,* vol. VII, "Society and Solitude," p. 41–59. [Houghton, Mifflin and Co., Boston & New York; The Riverside Press, Cambridge, Mass., 1870]). Also cf. Plato's comment that "those things which are said to be done by Nature are indeed done by Divine Art." A number of fine treatises and essays dealing with speculations regarding the essential nature of art have been published over the years including *Sacred and Profane Beauty: The Holy in Art* by Gerardus van der Leeuw (New York, Chicago: Holt, Rinehart and Winston, 1963) and *Art, Creativity and the Sacred,* edited by Diane Apostolos-Cappadona (New York: Crossroad, 1989).

18   *Genesis* 3:5–6.

19   See Ralph Waldo Emerson's essay "Art." This quote from p. 55.

20   The other dark arts coupled with blackened magic might also be explored but that is a seductive field and potentially dangerous territory that will be left for another excursion into the mystic realms.

21   Elements for these observations were first published in *Festina Lente: A Celebration of the Wosk–McDonald Aldine Collection at Simon Fraser University,* published by SFU Friends of the Library & The Alcuin Society, 1996. A second source was from an email addressed to Leah Gordon, August 24, 2005 that was quoted in the *Alcuin Society* catalogue for *Awards for Excellence in Book Design in Canada* (September 2005). A version of the Tetsugen story can be found in *Zen Flesh, Zen Bones,* compiled by Paul Reps and Nyogen Senzaki, originally printed by Tuttle Publishing in 1957.

22   It posited two original and opposing forces, that of *Ahura Mazda* (Light and Goodness) in an eternal clash with *Ahriman* (Darkness and Evil).

23   The Torah, for example, depicts life in this world as a battleground between conflicting forces: "Today I have given you the choice between life and death, between blessings and curses. Now I call on heaven and earth to witness the choice you make. Therefore choose life, so that you and your descendants might live!" (*Deut.* 30:19)

24   A fundamental aspect of human consciousness is self-reflective awareness. Everywhere we go, our inner critic—along with a hundred other characteristics—is there. This faculty comes with a warning, for if we critique ourselves too obsessively we may descend into darkness and paralyzing anxiety.

25   In addition to training critics, we also need to educate society on how to react to the opinions of others. When we recover from our wounds, we may realize that the

purpose of criticism is to enlighten and advance us. Initially it may be painful but the Wisdom Traditions suggest that any love that does not include correction is false and that a thoughtful person appreciates appropriate criticism because it leads to improvement. This sentiment is expressed in the statement from *Proverbs* 9:8 — "Do not rebuke mockers or they will hate you; rebuke the wise and they will love you."

26   Cf. *In Praise of Shadows* by Junichiro Tanizaki, Vintage Books, London (2001), originally published in Japan, 1933; first English translation, 1977. This classic essay on Japanese aesthetics is a paean to dim light, shadows and darkness. It juxtaposes "the collision between the shadows of traditional Japanese interiors with the dazzling light of the modern age."

27   *Psalms* 115: 5-7.

28   The Book of Deuteronomy reminds us that "It is not in heaven that you should need to ask, 'Who will ascend into heaven to get it for us and proclaim it so that we may do it?' Neither is it beyond the sea that you should need to ask, 'Who will cross the sea to get it for us that we may hear it and do it?' But the word is very near to you; it is in your mouth and in your heart, so that you may do it" (*Deut.* 30: 11-14). The Koran strikingly states that Allah is closer to a person than their own jugular vein (*Surah* 50:16).

29   A variant originally appeared in the article "Museum as Metaphor and Matter: A Preface to the Jewish Museum & Archives of British Columbia" by Yosef Wosk in the *Commemorative Book* celebrating the inauguration of the Jewish Museum & Archives of British Columbia, *Jewish Historical Society of B.C.*, p. 25-28, (March 2007). It was later edited and laid out to resemble a chalice, entitled *Museum as Matter and Metaphor,* and prepared as a keepsake designed by Robert Reid and Yosef Wosk for the Canadian Museums Association Annual Conference, Toronto, 2009. 500 copies were printed in Vancouver by David Clifford at the Black Stone Press on paper handmade by Reg Lissel. The poem appeared in a second keepsake for the Museum of Vancouver Legacy Dinner, October 6, 2014; 218 copies printed by David Clifford at the Black Stone Press on Arches 90 lb. mould made paper. The title for that iteration was *Museum as Matter and Metaphor: Observations from a contemplative stroll in an archetypal garden* by Yosef b'R Moshe Aharon Ha'Levi.

30   *Habakkuk* 2:14.

31   "We shall not cease from exploration / And the end of all our exploring / Will be to arrive where we started / And know the place for the first time" (T. S. Eliot, from "Little Gidding," *Four Quartets*; originally published 1943). Also cf. *The Hero with a Thousand Faces* by Joseph Campbell (Pantheon Books, 1949) as an analytical study of the hero's journey monomyth. It, in turn, was influenced by the work of Carl Jung. Also see two of numerous world stories that convey this message: *The Happiest Man in the World,* a traditional Sufi story as transmitted by Idries Shah, and the Jewish folktale, *The Treasure,* as told and illustrated by Uri Shulevitz.

32   *Midrash* on *Ecclesiastes* 1:13.

33   *Pirkei Avot* 2:21; 2nd century CE.

34   Some people worship knowledge, using it as a weapon or as a symbol of status and power. It is good to appreciate this way of perceiving reality but not to be enslaved by it nor make it into a false idol. In 1709 Alexander Pope composed a poem, *An Essay on Criticism*, that contained these enduring words: "A little learning is a dangerous thing; drink deep, or taste not the Pierian spring: there shallow draughts intoxicate the brain, and drinking largely sobers us again." To which Einstein (1879–1955) responded: "A little knowledge is a dangerous thing. So is a lot."

35   Fermentation adds flavour while giving time to break down some of the sugars and starches, making them easier to digest while also increasing the availability of vitamins and minerals for our bodies to absorb. The leavening action in dough is also an appropriate metaphor. These transformative processes are similar to the maturation of information into knowledge and eventually into wisdom.

36   Examples of this are the Australian Aboriginal Dreamtime and the biblical Sabbath, the ability to live and work for six days but to know how to then take a day off from relentless activity and consumption, to rest and re-soul on the seventh. You don't have to wait for the weekend to take time off. Any moment can be liberated from the incessant parade of what is often self-imposed modern slavery. Take a moment, any moment, this moment, to declare your freedom from innovation, from action, from deadlines. This is not another imposed deadline but rather a lifeline—a gift of expansive breath in the midst of reliance on alleged technological imperatives.

37   "Verse" is sometimes translated as "poem." The excerpt is from Rilke's novel, *The Notebooks of Malte Laurids Brigge,* originally published in 1910. There have been a number of translations from the German into English including that by M. D. Herter Norton (New York: W. W. Norton & Company, 1949) and Stephen Mitchell (New York: Random House, 1983). Only the final paragraph of this exquisite meditation is included here. It is worth searching for the full quote in print or online.

38   *A Meditation on Small and Large Museums* by Stephen E. Weil (Washington: Smithsonian Institution Press, 1990). See New York Times online obituary for more background as to Weil's significant contributions to museums, law and the arts. Another of his seminal publications was *Making Museums Matter* (Washington: Smithsonian Books, 2002). Although many museums are beginning to serve a role closer to the centre of civic life, they still seem to be in the "nice to have" category rather than being elevated to "essential services" status (see Elaine Heumann Gurian, BC Museums Association conference speaker, 2005).

39   Lyrics from the song *Knockin' On Heaven's Door* originally written and recorded by Bob Dylan for the soundtrack of the 1973 film *Pat Garrett and Billy the Kid;* subsequently covered by others including Guns N' Roses, 1990.

40   Most recent estimates suggest that the age of the *known* universe is 13.8 billion years old. Its approximate size spans a distance of 93 billion light years. These

estimates will continue to be revised as more powerful scientific instruments are invented to gather and interpret data.

41   From front flap of Mumford's *The Myth of the Machine: Technics & Human Development* (London: Secker & Warburg, 1967).

42   *Genesis* 1:26–27; 5:1; 9:6.

43   See *Really Useful: The Origins of Everyday Things* by Joel Levy (Collingdale, PA.: Diane Publishing Company, 2002). In his introduction, Levy writes (albeit with a Eurocentric bias): "Many everyday objects have surprisingly long histories, dating back to the dawn of civilization.... Their development often follows a pattern: Invented by the ancient Egyptians or Babylonians, perfected by the Greeks and Romans, lost in the Dark Ages, and rediscovered in the Middle Ages, mechanized and electrified by the Victorians, and mass-produced in the 20th century."

The continuing Industrial Revolution of mass-produced goods made them affordable to almost everyone, so much so that we are now "the consumer generation" and have had to learn to deal with our own excess including storage, garbage and pollution so significant that it is causing global climate change. This has led to inventive storage as well as advanced organizational systems and recycling technologies but also to obesity and massive clean-up operations.

As technologies progressed, products became easier to manufacture, less expensive and were more readily available to all. There was also a democratization of knowledge (witness the 15th Century's Gutenberg Revolution and the present computer revolution) and a parallel shift in political power from royalty to nobles to the people. A clever cartoon depicting the tension of this transfer depicts England's King Arthur sitting with his knights at the Round Table, purportedly as equals. The caption, however, belies the illusion as the king proclaims: "It is true that we are all equal, but by dint of my crown and sceptre I am just a little more equal than the rest of you" (unknown source; c. 1998).

Buckminster Fuller gave pithy expression to this evolution towards equalization when he described the world as "Spaceship Earth with first class accommodations for all". See Fuller's *Operating Manual for Spaceship Earth* (Carbondale: Southern Illinois University Press, 1968) and (New York: Simon and Schuster, 1969).

There may be various modes of democratization and Declarations of Human Rights, but draconian measures of forced equality have never proven successful. Under what turned out to be dictatorial Communist regimes, most notably in twentieth-century Russia and China, perhaps as many as 110 million people were killed in the name of socially engineered equality.

44   London: Pan Books, 1979.

45   Quoting Fit the Seventh from the original Hitchhiker radio series, on Christmas Eve, 1978. Also found in Geoffrey Perkins and Douglas Adams, *The Hitchhiker's Guide to the Galaxy: The Original Radio Scripts* (London: Pan Books, 1985).

46   These Ten Elemental Principles appear in a multitude of guises. They are further complimented by the Four Worlds of Kabbalah, the Jewish mystical tradition,

where they are described as the realms of *Asiyah* Physical Action, *Yetzirah* Emotion, *Beriah* Intellect, and *Atzilut* Spirit. Much study is required to comprehend these esoteric teachings. Not everyone who searches is granted understanding. In one Buddhist text, the Buddha—in his fully realized consciousness—described himself as "the elder brother of the universe," i.e. identified with the Primordial Principle preceding creation. For a cursory review of the origins of the idea of technology, see Evan Scherr's online posting "The Origin of the Word Technology" (February 16, 2014).

47   Diane Ackerman, *The Moon by Whale Light and other adventures among bats, penguins, crocodilians, and whales,* p. 131 (New York: Vintage Books, a division of Random House, 1992).

48   For an article on Criswell and a short video of his famous introduction to *Plan 9 from Outer Space,* see Wikipedia's "The Amazing Criswell."

49   This has been a well-debated concept through various civilizations and centuries. Cf. a number of online articles including the Physics Central presentation: "How was the universe created if physics states matter can neither be created nor destroyed?"; "The Conservation of Mass-Energy"; also "Conservation of mass," and the Wikipedia article on "Conservation of energy."

50   Some of these characterizations are from the article "Opinion: Why I Hate Museums" by James Durston, published online under CNN Travel, August 22, 2013. My daughter, Rahel Wosk, has also passionately expressed similar viewpoints.

51   Is that the appropriate word—patrons—to describe those whom we serve? It's not patients but perhaps it could be clients or guests? Or perhaps even friends? When speaking of libraries—something that is equally applicable to museums—John Ralston Saul commented: "You do not have a commercial relationship with those you serve. Your job is not to serve *clients.* Libraries build a relationship between books and *citizens*" (*Feliciter,* July/August 1998, p. 33).

52   Could not find the source for this quote.

53   See *The Global Brain: Speculations on the evolutionary leap to planetary consciousness* by Peter Russell (Los Angeles: JP Tarcher, 1983) and related YouTube video. Also refer to the Wikipedia article "Global brain" and its numerous related links.

54   Along with our greatly expanded sense of place and space, we now realize that there is no up or down except in relative terms. I first recognized this on an expedition to the South Pole in 2012. On a tour of the U.S. scientific research outpost, the Amundsen–Scott South Pole Station, we visited the library. I noticed a globe of the world with the South Pole turned upwards, a position that we usually associate with the North. I continued to contemplate this illusion until I had the opportunity to ask the Canadian astronaut, Chris Hadfield, whether there was an objective sense of direction in outer space or was it just an Earth bias—or more correctly, a northern hemispheric civilizational bias—that declared North as up and South as down.

He corroborated my observations that there is no objective up or down in space; it is determined as needed and is a relativistic calculation. A third confirmation was gleaned in conversation with a nuclear physicist.

55   Thomas Berry, *The New Story: Comments on the Origin, Identification, and Transmission of Values,* first published in *Teilhard Studies,* Number 1 (Winter 1978).

56   Woody Allen, "My Speech to the Graduates", New York Times, August 10, 1975, p. 25. The full speech can be accessed online.

57   Walt Whitman (1819–1892), *Song of Myself,* 51. The poem is included in his masterpiece, the often-revised book of collected poetry, *Leaves of Grass.*

58   Further thoughts on this subject are found in the book *Futuretainment: Yesterday the World Changed, Now it's your turn* by Mike Walsh (London and New York: Phaidon Press, 2009). In his opening manifesto, Walsh states that "digital distribution was taking all the familiar formats of media such as music, movies, television and games and turning them into something more fluid, something that consumers could play with." We witnessed the birth of the Interactive digital revolution and are increasingly engulfed by it. Technologies are no longer a one-way linear conversation. Digital media is getting closer to total immersion, as in Artificial Intelligence and brain–technology interfacials. Much is already wireless—you no longer need an instrument, a record, cassette or compact disc, not even a book, nor do you have to go to the store to buy one. All kinds of information in multiple formats serving every sense are now instantaneously available online. They transcend time and cause space to disappear. "In a world where every piece of content is available to anyone at any time, there is no need for broadcast towers to beam everything out.… People start to rely on a different kind of network: an Audience Network." It is on demand, anywhere, anytime, responsive and smarter than ever before. "Why believe mainstream marketers who tell you what is worthy of your attention when your friends are a far more reliable source of information?"

For the new generation "digital media is not something new, it is entirely natural." Consequently, I would advise every museum to not only have professional staff and a board of directors but also a Youth Council, those who surf the Net with abandon and inhabit the leading edge of evolution.

59   American Association of Museums, *Museum News,* March/April 1997, p. 31. "To Be There or Not to Be There: Presence, Telepresence, and the Future of Museums" by William J. Mitchell and Oliver B. R. Strimpel.

60   They define the downsides of *High Presence,* i.e. actually visiting the site, as high cost, fixed location, limited opening hours and numbers of visitors, navigation on foot and exhibit limited to present on-site collection. The benefits include aura of the original artefact, true scale, unlimited detail, group experience and contextualization. The benefits of the *Low Presence* virtual visit are low cost, flexible locations, always open, unlimited number of visitors but never crowded, hyperlink navigation, and the visitor can combine resources from many other sites thereby enhancing information. Some of the downsides of virtual visits are that the aura of

encountering original artefacts is lost, the scale and texture are diminished, it is an individual experience and often decontextualized.

61   A similar sentiment was expressed in the article "In Revamped Library Schools, Information Trumps Books" (*The Chronicle of Higher Education*, April 7, 2000, p. A43).
Officials at the University of Michigan's School of Information "felt there was a need for a new professional with the technological prowess of a computer scientist but the heart and soul of a librarian." "The amount of electronic information is doubling every 60 minutes," says John King, dean of Michigan's School of Information. "How do you decide what to keep and what not? What is the value of the information?" One handheld device can access far more print publications, pictures or film than the largest material library or museum could ever hold. However, this electronic amplification of information does not negate many earlier technologies, for each retains its unique veracity of experience.

62   *BrainWorld* Magazine, thematic issue on The Future. Issue 1, Volume 10, Fall 2018.

63   *Ibid*. p. 58. This estimate of atoms in the universe is very low. According to another source (*www.universetoday.com/36302/atoms-in-the-universe*) the equation is exponentially greater: "It is estimated that there are between $10^{78}$ to $10^{82}$ atoms in the known, observable universe. In layman's terms that works out to between ten quadrillion vigintillion and one-hundred thousand quadrillion vigintillion atoms."

64   *Genesis* 3:1-15.

65   See the online article on Mentalfloss.com: "Early Trains Were Thought to Make Women's Uteruses Fly Out" by Janet Burns, August 26, 2015.

66   From the *Bhagavata Purana*. This is a small excerpt from a longer and fascinating story. See online for a number of versions in various languages, including Hindi, as well as illustrations and animated productions.

67   The neighbourhood is no longer just a few blocks long but rather the Whole Earth. In the early-16th century, the Copernican realignment demonstrated that Earth was no longer the centre of the Solar System but rather a mid-size planet revolving around an average star, one of over a hundred billion in our galaxy that we named the Milky Way. (By attaching names to things we generate the illusion that we have defined, tamed and owned them). When we sent extra-terrestrial telescopes into space, we discovered that the cosmos was thousands of times larger than we once thought and we were humbled, once again, to accept that our galaxy is a speck of dust, just one of billions more in an expanding material universe.

68   The shelf life of most electronic products today is only a few months and you can be assured that the only reason the next innovation is not already at market is because the consumer—already inundated with products—would not be able to

keep up with the inventors and manufacturers. I remember, about thirty years ago, suffering from culture shock for the first time when I took a broken radio in for repair. The technician took one look at it and advised me that it would cost more to fix it than to just purchase a new one. I was confused for I was of the generation that fixed and kept things. Now we have planned obsolescence built into our system, but at least there is a proliferation of recycling programs and the recent emergence of Repair Cafés.

69   William Morris (1834–1896): "Have nothing in your house that you do not know to be useful, or believe to be beautiful."

70   "1998 CLA Annual Conference—Inaugural Address," by Sydney Jones; *Feliciter*, July/August 1998.

71   From the back cover. *In Praise of Shadows* by Junichiro Tanizaki, translated from the Japanese by Thomas J. Harper and Edward G. Seidensticker (London: Vintage Books, 1977 and 2001).

72   Commonly spelled *ouroboros* or *uroboros*; from the Greek, a compound of *ourá*—"tail", and *bóros*—"devouring" or "swallowing." It is "a circular symbol depicting a snake, or less commonly a dragon, swallowing its tail, as an emblem of wholeness or infinity" (*Oxford Dictionary*). An ancient archetype, Jung referred to it as "a dramatic symbol for the integration and assimilation of the opposite, i.e. of the shadow" (*Mysterium Coniunctionis*). Helpful video presentations about the symbolic idea of Ouroboros can be found online including *www.youtube.com/@mysteryscroll/videos1*; for a speculative view that operates between science and symbolism see *youtube.com/watch?v=qsGv_HyhEM4*.

73   "next spring" from *Breathin' My Name with a Sigh* (1981).

74   *Ex*. 3:8; *Nu*. 14:8; *Deut*. 31:20; *Ez*. 20:15. Cf. *Ketuvot* 11b, "milk flows from the goats' [udders] and honey drips from the figs [and dates]".

75   Wine—an intoxicating, heady and impregnating liquid—represents the male principle; bread—associated more with nurturing, the body and the earth—is symbolic of the female principle.

76   "Earth thickens and attracts; water breaks down and purifies; air makes fluid and dries; fire divides and completes" (Johann J. Becher [1635–1682], *Opuscula chymica*).

77   In addition to modern science, a number of traditional sources caution consequences including *Lev*. 18:25–28; *Lev*. 20:22; *Is*. 24:5; *Jer*. 12:4.

78   Douglas Adams, *The Restaurant at the End of the Universe* (1980), second volume in *The Hitchhiker's Guide to the Galaxy* comedy science fiction trilogy.

79   *Nikhnas ya'yin, yo'tsai sod*—"Wine enters; secrets emerge;" *In vino veritas*—"In wine there is truth."

80   Yiddish, meaning "Eat, eat, my child."

81   See Franz Kafka, "My Destination," from *Parables and Paradoxes*.

82   See *Conference of the Birds* by Farid ud-Din Attar, twelfth century Persian mystic poet.

83   We could include time in the womb (9 months) to the calculation and even add three months as a bonus for "time served" as a birthday present. That would allow us to celebrate being one year old on our day of birth. Others may choose to only count from when a fetus is considered a person. The pre-natal drama is so fraught with legal, ethical, religious and medical circumstances that perhaps it is best to leave our calculations as we currently count, i.e. from the moment of actual birth. Some cultures, such as South Korea and China, use different age-counting systems. They consider the child to be one year old at the time of their birth and another year older on the day of the New Year, not their personal day of birth. These systems of counting, however, are only used for cultural and social purposes, not for legal applications such as voting or driving.

84   It seems to be part of our self-reflective nature that we are not only aware of ourselves but are also aware of being aware of ourselves *ad infinitum*. We observe not just the immediate moment but are also captive in the funfair Hall of Mirrors of Consciousness. It is where Imagination transcends Measurement.

85   In response to my musings, Gareth Sirotnik, a friend and Zen practitioner, wrote: "Your reflections on measurement remind me there's another way to measure time and space: *just this*. Just this instant of time and space. And this *this* is forever, the one constant. No matter what arbitrary system we use for measuring the apparent passing of time and space, there is always *Just This*. Maybe one could call this *this* God; or not. To savour *just this*."

86   Cf. Charles Dickens, *A Tale of Two Cities* (1859): "It was the best of times, it was the worst of times, it was the age of wisdom, it was the age of foolishness, it was the epoch of belief, it was the epoch of incredulity, it was the season of Light, it was the season of Darkness, it was the spring of hope, it was the winter of despair, we had everything before us, we had nothing before us …."

87   *Ecclesiastes* (*Kohelet*) 1:7. Elie Wiesel took the title for his two-volume autobiography from this verse. It also reflects nature's deep ecological cycle. Although unrelated, this brings to mind an inspiring quote by Rabbi Yohanan ben Zakkai in the 1st century CE: "If all the heavens were parchment, all the trees quills, and all the oceans ink, they would not suffice to record the wisdom that I learned from my masters. And yet I took away from them no more than an insect takes when it dips in the sea."

88   Groucho Marx was quoted as saying: "Those are my principles. If you don't like them, I've got others."

89   See the poem by Robert Burns (1785), *To a Mouse, on Turning Her Up in Her Nest With the Plough, November, 1785*:
     But, Mousie, thou art no thy-lane [you are not alone],

In proving foresight may be vain;
The best-laid schemes o' mice an' men
Gang aft agley [Often go askew].

90   There are also a number of philosophical, spiritual and scientific cosmological theories that postulate the eternality of time and space, i.e. that the Universe exists forever.

91   "Then [Moses] said, "I beseech you, show me your glory" (*Exodus* 33:18).

92   "Now if I [Moses] have found favour in Your sight, please, let me know Your ways" (*Exodus* 33:13).

93   There are a number of allusions to seeing the Face of God in biblical literature. They are to be taken metaphorically since the true essence of a non-corporeal deity has no physical visage. Some examples are *Gen.* 32:30, *Ex.* 24:10, *Deut.* 34:10, *Ezekiel* 1:28; *Ezek.* 43:3.

94   *Ex.* 3: 13–15. "Then Moses asked God, "Suppose I go to the Israelites and say to them, 'The God of your fathers has sent me to you,' and they ask me, 'What is His name?' What should I tell them?" God said to Moses, "I AM WHO I AM (*Ehyeh Asher Ehyeh*). This is what you are to say to the Israelites: 'I AM has sent me to you.'" God also told Moses, "Say to the Israelites, 'The LORD, the God of your fathers—the God of Abraham, the God of Isaac, and the God of Jacob—has sent me to you.' This is My name forever, and this is how I am to be remembered in every generation." Also see Note 104 below regarding names.

95   *Exodus 33.* Using human physical attributes such as "hand" and "back" are symbolic metaphors, a linguistic conceit, a vehicle to assist our understanding and help translate an experience of the non-corporeal into a material world.

96   Even a *yeridah,* a descent or falling out, is an opportunity to learn from the mistake—to mine the depths, to explore the dungeon, to become sensitized to territory (physical, emotional, intellectual or spiritual) you may never have visited—and to then arise and carry on. No personality in the Torah is presented as being perfect; everyone had flaws and yet they persisted. In a *midrash,* King David is quoted as saying, "If I did not fall, I would never have gotten up. If one falls a hundred times, then get up a hundred and one."

97   See "Bible Verses About Eagles" on the *Bible Study Tools* website. I have also been fortunate to live among eagles on Bowen Island and to know Haida master carver, James Hart, hereditary chief of the Eagle Clan on Haida Gwaii. I look forward to learning more of their traditional wisdom—the eagle, the land, the waters, the people and their stories.

98   *Sanhedrin* 99a.

99   According to tradition, David lived exactly seventy years; he was born and died on *Shavuot,* the Festival of Weeks or Pentecost. *Shavuot* is celebrated on the

50th day (Pentecost, from the Greek pentēkostē—50th), or seven weeks, after Passover. It is both a harvest festival and the anniversary of the revelation of the Torah on Mt. Sinai.

100  For example, the premise of reward and punishment: In the ideal world, the Torah suggests that if one follows the *mitsvot,* commandments (divine directives), and lives a moral life, then one will be rewarded with peace in the land and a long healthy life with family. If the directives were ignored, then all would be cursed and cut off, disease would be rampant and exile would be the final result.

When this did not always work out according to the neat action/reaction formula, rabbinic theology extended the framework to include a World to Come. This doubled the parameters of the biblical doctrine of reward and punishment. Now you could have four basic categories: 1) Someone who was righteous but suffered in this world would be accorded their reward in *Olam Ha'Bah,* the World to Come; 2) those who were evil and yet prospered in this world would be punished in the next; 3) those who were righteous and enjoyed this world received their reward in both this and the World to Come; 4) those who were evil and suffered in this world, were punished in both realms.

We should also discuss reconciling the apparently contradictory statements of *Ha'kol b'yedai Shamayim hutz mai'Yirat Shamayim,* "everything is in the hands of heaven except for the Fear of Heaven," and *Ha'kol b'yedai Shamayim hutz mai'tzinim u'pahim,* "everything is in the hands of heaven except for colds and fevers."

101  When I was a child, I talked like a child, I thought like a child, I reasoned like a child. When I became a man, I set aside childish ways (1 *Corinthians* 13:11). Also cf. *John* 21:18.

102  I have been fortunate to visit over a hundred countries as well as a thousand provinces, states and cities on all seven continents. I've been on expeditions to both the North and South Poles and have circumnavigated the Earth five times: Once by air, twice by ship, and—this is a trick answer—twice by foot (walking around the poles). I became a Fellow of the Royal Canadian Geographical Society and prepared a publication on psychogeography, the correspondence between our physical bodies, consciousness and geography.

103  In spite of almost never finding learning or examinations easy, I discovered that I possessed three crucial characteristics: Curiosity, creativity and just enough discipline to complete most tasks. I often wanted to run away and abandon my studies. Instead, I learned to take short breaks and forced myself to study, to write, to complete the work even if it took me a few years longer than most. The principal environs where I lived and learned were Vancouver, Jerusalem, New York, Toronto, Philadelphia and Boston. Besides various certificates attesting to diverse fields of study, in the end and much to my surprise I earned a number of degrees: Two bachelors, two masters, two doctorates (along with another two honorary doctorates), and rabbinic ordination. My brother, Ken, once quipped: "You have so many degrees that you've got temperature," and "You've got more letters after your name than in it."

104  In a search for my real, not just given, name I've changed it a number of times. Even now, the name I bear seems to be just about used up. A rabbinic teaching suggests that when our parents name us, the name carries prophetic meaning and will influence our lives. As we mature into various aspects of our evolving selves, however, our names might also change. If a name is to be accurate then it must describe the essence of the object or subject. The Torah offers examples: *Genesis* 2:19-20 describes how after God had created all the animals "He brought them to the man to see what he would name them; and whatever the man called each living creature, that was its name. So the man gave names to all the livestock, the birds in the sky and all the wild animals." An interpretation informs us that Adam looked into the essence of each creature and recognized its true name. People still take great pleasure in naming; scientists, especially, have ordered the world according to nomenclature. Other biblical examples of name changes occurred when a *heh,* a letter from the divine name, was added to Avram as his spiritual personality matured. He became Avraham, Sarai became Sarah and Jacob became Yisrael. Your present name is your local or temporary handle; one also possesses a universal name although it is much more difficult to discern. Then there is the Ineffable Name of God, one that cannot even be pronounced. The Creator, however, does have many familiar names. Islam identifies the 99 Names of Allah. According to the Kabbalah, the entire Torah is nothing but the names of God.

105  "For now we see through a glass, darkly; but then face to face: now I know in part; but then shall I know even as also I am known" (1 *Corinthians* 13:12).

106  Three years later, Audain's frankly revealing memoir was published as *One Man in His Time* (Douglas & McIntyre, 2022). The publisher described the book as "The unlikely and riveting story of how a left-wing activist became one of BC's most accomplished business leaders and philanthropists, championing projects in the visual arts and innovation in Canadian wildlife protection and sustainability. Freedom rider. Student radical. Academic. Social activist. Residential developer. Museum builder. Grizzly bear protector. Michael Audain has been all of these things and more in a colourful life spanning eight decades, three continents and five careers. Born into a branch of the legendary BC Dunsmuir clan that had lost its wealth and social status, little was expected of Audain. A lonely teenager plagued by insecurities, he was a dismal failure in the classroom and on the playing field. Yet Audain would become one of the most prominent home builders in British Columbia and a well-known philanthropist in support of the visual arts and wildlife causes." *BC BookWorld* lauded the publication as "a brave and often audacious memoir … a thoroughly original book about a vital builder of British Columbia."

107  "If you see your fellow Israelite's ox or sheep straying, do not ignore it but be sure to take it back to its owner. If they do not live near you or if you do not know who owns it, take it home with you and keep it until they come looking for it. Then give it back. Do the same if you find their donkey or cloak or anything else they have lost. Do not ignore it" (*Deut.* 22:1-4). And also compare: "If you come across your enemy's ox or donkey wandering off, be sure to return it. If you see the

donkey of someone who hates you fallen down under its load, do not leave it there; be sure you help them with it" (*Ex.* 23:4-5).

108  A rabbinic commentary suggests that Moses argued with God at the Burning Bush for seven days and seven nights to not choose him but to rather send someone else to liberate the people. Many other prophets were equally demurring, among them Jonah who tried to hide from the prophetic calling and Amos who declared "I am not a prophet nor the son of a prophet" (*Amos* 7:14).

109  See *Matthew* 7:15-20 (also cf. *Matt.* 12:33 and *Luke* 6:43–45).

Beware of false prophets who come to you in sheep's clothing, but inwardly they are ferocious wolves. You shall know them by their fruits. Do people gather grapes from thornbushes or figs from thistles? Likewise, every good tree brings forth good fruit; but a corrupt tree brings forth evil fruit. A good tree cannot bear bad fruit, neither can a bad tree bring forth good fruit. Every tree that does not bring forth good fruit is cut down and cast into the fire. Therefore, by their fruit you shall know them.

110  Envisioned by Haida master carver and hereditary chief of the Eagle Clan, James Hart, "The Dance Screen (The Scream Too)" was inaugurated on September 22, 2018 at the Audain Art Museum in Whistler, B.C.

111  I cannot remember the source for the following reflections on Hugo; perhaps it was a page on the Internet: Hugo (Feb. 26, 1802–May 22, 1885) did no less than participate in the formation of modern France. His remarkable life spanned two monarchies, two republics, two revolutions and two empires. As a statesman and a writer, he embodied liberal ideas and gave voice to the downtrodden, achieving the rare quality of being both a patriot and a humanist. In stature, he 'was to France what Queen Victoria was to England', writes Hugo's biographer Graham Robb. The French newspaper *Le Figaro* declared his funeral 'the death knell of a century that is ending'. His coffin lay in state under the Arc de Triomphe and was buried in the Panthéon, surrounded by the heroes of the republic.

112  *Ecclesiastes* 7:20; and see *Romans* 3:10.

113  The Museum of Anthropology at the University of British Columbia. The largest teaching museum in Canada, MOA "has been at the forefront of bringing Indigenous art into the mainstream by collecting and curating traditional and contemporary Indigenous art in a way that respects the artists and the cultures from which this work comes."

114  From *Hebrew Verse*, edited and translated by T. Carmi, New York, Penguin, 1981.

115  The original *Letter to Michael* quoted the entirety of No. 2 of the *Four Quarters* but for reasons of both length and copyright issues only the final stanza is quoted herein. The full poem is available in numerous print editions as well as on the Internet.

116 "The Lord God took the man and put him in the Garden of Eden to work it and to guard it" (*Gen.* 2:15).

117 A number of religious traditions direct their adherents to uproot themselves—at least temporarily—so they can experience the lessons of exile. Sometimes one must alter external circumstances to facilitate inner journeys. The initial recorded communications of God with Abraham, the first Hebrew, were instructions to *Laikh lekhah*, "Go; leave your land, your birthplace and your father's house" (*Genesis* 12:1). After the Exodus from Egypt, the nation of liberated slaves journeyed through the desert for forty years (i.e. an entire generation, for it takes a long time to learn how to be free). Jesus, himself an itinerant teacher, called his disciples from their mundane, settled lives to dedicate themselves to a greater purpose. Many Hindu sadhus dedicate their lives to sacred roaming; some Buddhist as well as Christian monks, nuns and ascetics may spend years in voluntary poverty and wandering with almost no possessions. They rely on the charity of the villagers for food and other necessities. Every religion also has its pilgrimages, opportunities for its practitioners, at least temporarily, to fulfill the sacred directive to wander in search of the divine.

118 "The bashful [i.e. one who is afraid to ask, to seek, to search] cannot learn, and the impatient should not teach" (*Pirkei Avot* 2:6).

119 Learning how to receive is as important as learning how to give. Opportunities present themselves to us constantly; we, however, spend most of our time in a kind of convoluted state of denial. On the one hand, we wish, pray and work towards an imagined goal; on the other hand, when the wished-for desire appears—often clothed in the surprising guise of unexpected characters and circumstances—we often run, hide or excuse ourselves from the invitation. Just as the Earth absorbs rain, so, too, the student can absorb teaching. The heart is similarly filled with empathy, the bowl is open to its contents, and the labourer receives his wages. The Jewish mystical tradition is known as *Kabbalah*: the word itself translates as "receiving," i.e. receiving the esoteric teachings as passed on through the generations.
An edifying Zen story describes the importance of emptying your cup so that you may be filled once again, as if for the first time.

> Nan-in, a Japanese master during the Meiji era (1868–1912), received a university professor who came to inquire about Zen.
> Nan-in served tea. He poured his visitor's cup full, and then kept on pouring. The professor watched the overflow until he could no longer restrain himself. "It is overfull. No more will go in!"
> "Like this cup," Nan-in said, "you are full of your own opinions and speculations. How can I show you Zen unless you first empty your cup?"

Found in various sources including *Zen Flesh, Zen Bones: A Collection of Zen and Pre-Zen Writings* by Paul Reps (Tuttle Publishing, North Clarendon, VT., 1957).

120 There are many references to this principle in world wisdom literature. A rather delightful modern iteration is the book *Steal Like an Artist: 10 Things Nobody*

*Told You About Being Creative* by Austin Kleon (Workman Publishing Company, New York, 2012). On a related note, T. S. Eliot wrote: "Immature poets imitate; mature poets steal; bad poets deface what they take, and good poets make it into something better, or at least something different. The good poet welds his theft into a whole of feeling which is unique, utterly different from that from which it was torn" (excerpt from Eliot's critical essay on Philip Massinger in *The Sacred Wood*).

The Maggid of Mezritch said: "Every lock has its key which is fitted to it and opens it. But there are strong thieves who know how to open without keys. They break the lock. So every mystery in the world can be unriddled by the particular kind of meditation fitted to it. But God loves the thief who breaks the lock open: I mean the man who breaks his heart for God" (*Tales of the Hasidim: The Early Masters*, Martin Buber, Schocken Books, 1949).

Also see the story of *Cutting the Gordian Knot* associated with Alexander the Great. It became "a proverbial term for a problem solvable only by bold action. In 333 BCE, Alexander the Great, on his march through Anatolia, reached Gordium, the capital of Phrygia. There he was shown the chariot of the ancient founder of the city, Gordius, with its yoke lashed to the pole by means of an intricate knot with its end hidden. According to tradition, this knot was to be untied only by the future conqueror of Asia.... Alexander sliced through the knot with his sword, but, in earlier versions, he found the ends either by cutting into the knot or by drawing out the pole. The phrase 'cutting the Gordian knot' has thus come to denote a bold solution to a complicated problem" (*britannica.com/topic/Gordian-knot*).

121 Literally translated as "jealousy of the scribes," but to grasp its intention, the full term *kinat sofrim tarbeh hokhmah* (*Baba Batra* 21b) is better translated as "competition among scholars increases wisdom." The term *kinah*, "jealousy," is found in a number of earlier biblical sources such as *Ex.* 20:2-4, *ibid.* 34.14, *Deut.* 32:16, and *Isa.* 11:13. In a second century rabbinic mishnah, its pernicious quality is reinforced: "Jealousy, lust and honour remove one from this world" (*Pirkei Avot* 4:21). The positive application of potentially negative traits is a well-known, if somewhat dangerous, pedagogic technique.

122 This will stimulate your learning and help propel you to the next level. This kind of stealing knowledge—*not* academic plagiarism—is permitted by the great teachers of Eastern and Western esoteric traditions who understood that not everything could be transmitted rationally from teacher to student. Some things are too subtle, immaterial and intangible: they must be seized—or suddenly realized—by the student alone.

Classic Buddhist literature contains a number of examples of disciples who attained enlightenment in such ways. See *wikipedia.org/wiki/Enlightenment_in_Buddhism*, especially the section on "Sudden and gradual." These sudden transformations may be facilitated by master teachers but can only be completed after great discipline and sustained practice—and even then, almost accidentally—by the student.

123 Nachmanides, or Ramban (1194–1270), however, cautions dilettante students from wrongly supposing that they have uncovered the mysteries. He writes: "Now behold, I bring into a faithful covenant and give proper counsel to all who look into

this book not to reason or entertain any thought concerning any of the mystic hints which I write regarding the hidden matters of the Torah, for I do hereby firmly make known to him [the reader] that my words will not be comprehended nor known at all by any reasoning or contemplation, excepting *from the mouth of a wise Cabalist speaking into the ear of an understanding recipient.*" This translation is from "Torah on the Web–Virtual Beit Midrash" (*etzion.org.il/en/torah*) but also see *Ramban (Nachmanides): Commentary on the Torah,* especially his *Introduction to the Torah,* (Hebrew original first written in the mid-1200s and available in a number of editions including the important five volume English annotated translation by Charles B. Chavel, Shilo Publishing House, New York, 1971–1976).

124  "The Dark Illumination of Sat Hon," *Parabola,* Summer 2009, p. 48–55.

125  A fool, in its highest manifestation, is one who is given over completely to a spiritual belief or secular principle. We find examples among some of the prophets in ancient Israel, as well as dedicated adherents in Hinduism, Buddhism, Christianity, Islam, the North American First Nations and among shamanic traditions worldwide. In a modern secular or psychological sense, one could be a fool for an idea or a particular project. For some examples of "Fool Literature" see *The Feast of Fools: A Theological Essay on Festivity and Fantasy,* Harvey Cox (Perennial Library, Harper & Row, New York [by arrangement with Harvard University Press], 1969); *God's Fool: The Life and Times of Francis of Assisi,* Julien Green, translated from French by Peter Heinegg (Harper & Row, San Francisco, 1985); and *Holy Madness: Portraits of Tantric Siddhas,* Robert Linrothe, editor (Rubin Museum of Art, New York and Serindia Publishers, Chicago, 2006).

June McDaniel, in her work on the divine madness of the medieval *bhakti* saints in Bengal, also mentions other similar traditions: "Divine madness is not unique to Bengal, or even to India. It has been explored in various traditions: In both Eastern Orthodox and Western Christianity, among the Hasids of Eastern Europe, among the Sufis, in possession and trance dancers around the world." She then describes how Plato, in his dialogue *Phaedrus,* distinguished between pathological and divine manias and proceeded to list four types of divine madness: That which brings divination, that which opens one to possession trance, the third madness is the poetic, and the fourth, the erotic, which brings frenzied love. He then concluded "In reality, our greatest blessings come to us by way of madness, which indeed is a divine gift." (June McDaniel, *The Madness of the Saints: Ecstatic Religion in Bengal,* University of Chicago Press, 1989, p. 7.)

126  Using Tarot as a metaphorical guide, Janet Ossebaard describes *Le Mat,* The Fool, as a pilgrim on an open-ended journey that culminates as he is transformed into the inverted figure of the Hanged Man. She writes:

> According to the Tarot, the Fool is the card of infinite possibilities, total renewal, number zero and thus a new beginning. It also represents important decisions and optimism. The Fool is both the first and the last card, alpha and omega. He reminds us of sacred things that we have either forgotten or suppressed. He recognises his own ignorance and thus becomes the wisest of all. … In his search for his spiritual Self, the Fool

sits at the foot of a tree where he remains motionless for nine days. After nine days (there were nine days between the Fool and Transformation of Spirit into Matter) he rises and hangs upside down on one leg from a branch of the tree. He becomes the Tarot's Hanged Man. He completely surrenders and notices how his perception of the world starts to change. He floats between two worlds, the spiritual and the physical, and he can see both clearly. Suddenly, he sees all connections; mysteries unfold before him. The Fool is the last stage but one before the ultimate insight.

127 The Sacred Books of the East are nothing but words,
I looked through their covers one day sideways.
What Kabir talks of is only what he has lived through.
If you have not lived through something, it is not true.
(*Kabir: Ecstatic Poems,* English translation by Robert Bly, Beacon Press, Boston, [1976] 2007). Kabir (1440–1518), a mystic poet and saint of India, is uniquely revered by Hindu, Muslim and Sikh communities alike. Western spiritual seekers have now discovered his writings.

128 Usually we seek balance, symmetry and being centred. Evolving, vigorous vision, however, is most often achieved by breaking or transcending the images we have of ourselves. We may be afraid of making a mistake and so do nothing, or we may become calcified in a vain effort to maintain a particular posture that may have proved temporarily effective in the past. We can even morph into a state of autoidolatry where we may declare our dedication/allegiance to the ongoing exercise of "know thyself" but are, in fact, even more trapped in the deceptively safe act of self-worship. We become *comfort junkies:* We may realize that our addictive or negative traits need to change but it usually proves too much effort to evolve and most of us return to the comfort of our old habits. At times we need to fall or fly in order to look at things from a different perspective. Dare to be exiled to get a better view of paradise. We may then come to realize that we are no longer stuck in a narrow cage of conflicting dualities—right or wrong, black or white, this or that—but now inhabit a soaring universe of immense possibilities. Ultimately, however, in order to achieve a healthy balance (one that is characterized more as an ever-changing *dynamic balance* rather than a rigid *static state*), one must learn to live in paradox, to know the periphery as well as the centre, to become multivalent and what Jean Houston refers to as being a successful polyphrenic. (Houston described polyphrenia as a high-functioning, multi-levelled consciousness that is well-organized and synergistic within its levels.)

129 Whereas most of us are relatively scattered—the Zen folk refer to our overactive thoughts and inner chatter as *monkey mind*—and our powers dissipated, a dedicated fool can achieve much, often accomplishing what others consider impossible.

130 According to Rabbi Simcha Bunim of P'shiskha (1765–1827), everyone has two pockets, each containing a slip of paper. On one it is written "I am but dust and ashes," and on the other "The world was created just for me." Occasionally you

reach into one or the other pocket. The secret of living comes from knowing when to reach into which pocket.

The phrase *ve'anokhi afar va'eifar,* "I am but dust and ashes," was spoken by Abraham in conversation with God (*Genesis* 18:27). The concept of "the world was created just for me" originates in the mishnah *Sanhedrin* 4:5 and in the subsequent talmudic discourse in *Sanhedrin* 37a-b on the value of each person and the sanctity of life. The Talmud opines that "mankind was created as a single individual to teach you that anyone who destroys one ... life is considered by the Torah to have destroyed an entire world; and one who saves a ... life is considered by the Torah to have saved an entire world. And [another reason why we were created as a single individual was] because of people's nature, so that someone should not declare 'My ancestors were greater than yours.'"

131 Richard Buckminster "Bucky" Fuller (1895–1983), creator of the geodesic dome, was one of the most original thinkers of the 20th century. I had the good fortune to hear him speak on three occasions. At one of the gatherings—in Philadelphia in about 1981—I was able to spend some personal time with him and asked his permission to recite a rare Hebrew blessing on his behalf. The blessing is recited upon encountering an individual of great wisdom in a secular discipline. He looked at me, gave permission, slightly bowed his head and heard these words, first in Hebrew and then in English translation: "Blessed are You, Lord our God, Master of the Universe, who has given wisdom to flesh and blood." And the great man responded, "Amen." I recited that blessing only one other time, in 2007, when I was part of a delegation to Paris to meet the eminent Claude Lévi-Strauss (1908–2009). Travelling with me were the anthropologist Guy Buchholtzer and Kwakwaka'wakw (Kwakiutl) Chief William Cranmer. I represented the Canadian Academy of Independent Scholars and Lévi-Strauss, then almost 99 years old, had agreed to be our honorary patron along with John Ralston Saul. Deeply spiritual but not religious, he, too, consented, bowed his aged head filled with wisdom beyond measure, and received the venerable invocation.

132 He related that there was a time in his life when he was bankrupt and jobless, living in rundown housing and suffering terribly from the death of his young daughter. He blamed himself and this drove him to drink and to the verge of suicide. He told us how he stood on the docks overlooking Lake Michigan and, feeling worthless, was about to jump to an icy death.

133 Another favourite quote: "You never change things by fighting the existing reality. To change something, build a new model that makes the existing model obsolete." See the Internet for a cornucopia of pithy Fullerisms.

134 Oscar Wilde (1854–1900) once quipped "Be yourself; everyone else is already taken." Another of his relevant quotes: "Most people are other people. Their thoughts are someone else's opinions, their lives a mimicry, their passions a quotation" (*De Profundis*). An equally witty example, probably borrowed from Wilde, emerges from one of Charles Schulz's *Peanuts* comic strips (8-28) in which Lucy asks Snoopy "I've always wondered how you decided to become a dog." "That's a

good question," Snoopy replies. "I remember going down the list. Everything else was taken."

135   There is a difference between *authentic* humility and *false* humility. Authentic humility is when you know yourself and act accordingly; you do not self-aggrandize yourself but, when appropriate, you stand up tall and speak out loud. Moses, for example, was described as "the most humble person in the world" (*Numbers* 12:3) and yet he also learned—albeit reluctantly at first—to accept his mission, to organize his nation, to challenge a powerful kingdom, to stand up to rebellion, and even to negotiate with God. False humility, on the other hand, can be feigning a lack of vanity in an attempt to manipulate a particular situation. It can also indicate being stuck in a state of self-denial fuelled by fear: "Who am *I* to lead these people?" or "Who am *I* to accomplish that goal?" The emphasis is still on "I" and "me." In those instances, false humility is revealed to actually be a fearful survival tactic, an act of protective arrogance. I learned this concept from Rabbi Avraham Feigelstock.

136   Hebrew text from *Midrash Rabba, Gen.* 10:6. Just as there are times to pay attention to positive encouragement, there are also times to ignore negative criticism. If you *see* too much that it discourages you, become *blind*; if you *hear* others—or the echoes of your own doubts—tell you that you're incapable or that your quest is impossible, become *deaf* to their criticism; reach out to *touch* the sign that demands *Do Not Touch* and learn to cradle your distant dreams. Speak the words that no one else can say. Do not wait for Godot—the messianic proxy of your soulful yearnings—to achieve eschatological fulfilment. Do not fall prey to either flattery or indifference. Appreciate assistance; try to ignore those who would sabotage your goals. Persevere.

Of course there are exceptions to all these instructions—these well-meaning, hard-earned, common sense, erudite suggestions, for as Ecclesiastes (*Kohelet* 3:1-8) wrote so very long ago, "To everything there is a season, and a time to every purpose under heaven."

What is required is the wisdom to know the appropriate times to apply each principle, as Reinhold Niebuhr stated in his *Serenity Prayer*: "God, grant me the serenity to accept the things I cannot change, / Courage to change the things I can, / And wisdom to know the difference."

137   There is a difference between *creative destruction*, i.e. something that is purposeful and leads to improvement, versus a purely destructive act. For a fuller discussion based upon rabbinical definitions of labour on the Sabbath, see *ou.org/holidays/shabbat/the_concept_of_melachah*. Examples of creative destruction are editing, pruning, and recycling or demolishing a building to make way for a new one.

138   Although an entire civilization may seem like a chaotic collection of individual phenomena, it could also be appreciated—like a supergiant galaxy of a hundred trillion stars or the micromolecular structure of a common object—as a gestalt. It depends on the degree of perspective as one moves through macrocosmic and microcosmic modes of observation. The greatest *macrocosm* might be the universe itself (although one must also keep in mind that another Transcendent Reality may

"exist" beyond even that; beyond words, thought and metaphor; beyond all time and space, even transcending infinity that is dependent upon physical properties.) The trajectory towards the smallest *microcosm* may travel in the opposite direction but its conclusion is the same. Meanwhile, human beings (those temporary inhabitants of a bejewelled life-clinging planet) are endowed with self-reflective consciousness that can consider such thoughts. The Earth is awakening to *consciousness of itself* through its *human* mode of *being*.

On the other hand, we dare not arrogate consciousness as the unique prerogative of humanity. All that exists has consciousness: The rocks and minerals have their portion; vegetation absorbs and expresses its soulful share; as do the insects, birds, reptiles and mammals; fire, water, air and earth each relate to consciousness in their unique way. Consciousness, along with other forces, pervades the universe; we are merely its local iteration.

A single person is an entire world (*Sanhedrin* 4:8 [37a]). Our individual minds, like larger aggregates of human gatherings, contain multitudes of conflicting voices and creative—though often equally destructive—tendencies. At the other end of the spectrum, cultures and civilizations are merely amplifications of individual psyches engaged in interactive conversations. Civilization is the recapitulation of a single human being and, similarly, each individual encapsulates a cosmos. For further discussion see articles on *Recapitulation Theory*.

139  A civilization, like an individual, is not an absolute cosmic construct but rather one of innumerable potential manifestations.

140  See Aldous Huxley, *The Doors of Perception* and *Heaven and Hell* (Harper & Brothers, New York, [1954] 1956), and a number of other editions.

141  There are times when we must ignore the guardian and look past the barrier as just another obstacle to overcome. Some, when they see a wall, simply turn back. Others will try to pass to the left or explore the right. Some will climb over and others dig beneath or batter their heads, like Aries, against it until they are filled with scars and broken horns but at least they may have put a dent in the blockade, chipped away at the obstruction, or even broken through to the other side. Some may be talented enough to transform the opaque impediment into a translucent glow, a reflective mirror or even a transparent window but a window, no matter how clear, still suggests a boundary and limitation (*1 Cor.* 13:12). At times, some form of separation—coated lens to filter the sun, clothing against cold, lead to block radiation—may also serve as necessary protection (see *Ex.* 33:18-23). Then there are those searching for the path of least resistance or a mediated compromise who may abandon what is before them to examine alternate routes. Some great leaders, it is said, don't even see the wall. What is a barrier to some is an opportunity for others. These are the Masters of Creative Destruction.

Kafka expressed this liminal struggle best in *The Trial* where the doorkeeper does not permit the traveler to enter, not even the first of many gates. After waiting for too many years, and now upon his deathbed, the pilgrim is informed by the guardian, "No one else could ever be admitted here, since this gate was meant only for you. I am now going to shut it." (Franz Kafka, *The Trial,* Chapter Nine, "In the

Cathedral." The original German-language text, written in Prague in 1914, is available in a number of editions and various translations, including *The Trial: A New Translation Based on the Restored Text,* translated by Breon Mitchell [Schocken Books, New York, 1998]). Do not wait until you are dying to wish you had lived. We imagine that we are eternal (the mind can imagine eternity but the body cannot go along for the ride), and yet "life is like the shadow of a passing bird" (*Ps.* 144:4; *Ber. Rab.* 96).

There are portals that no one else can enter, and keys that no one else can hold, for doors that others cannot even see. Most of us become attached to the limited identities that we call ourselves and to narrow definitions that we mistake for reality. In an attempt to dismantle those limitations, I learned to live in multiple realms simultaneously. With some issues, I have had temporary success; with many others, I continue to stumble. Give yourselves permission. You have authority simply because you exist (cf. *Matt.* 21:23-27, *Mark* 11: 27-33, *Luke* 20:1-8).

And yet even if you do find your path and dare to enter the gate that was meant only for you, it is still not enough. There are others to nurture, a community to grow, friends to cultivate and family—whether by birth or by choice—to recognize as home. You are called upon to not only be yourself but to also demonstrate greatness of soul by identifying with others, by serving a purpose greater than yourself, more profound than your encapsulated ego. This intention may be at once boring and mundane but, at the same time, it is aware of and inspired by transcendent realms and a profusion of possibilities. See Hillel the Elder (c. 110 BCE–10 CE), who taught: "If I am not for myself, who will be for me? But if I am [only] for myself, what am I? And if not now, when?" (*Pirkei Avot* 1:14).

142 There are hundreds of examples of "the journey" in pilgrimage literature. My favourite description of the few who persevere is from the 12th century Persian writer Attar. In his *Conference of the Birds,* a Sufi epic poem of the Quest, he describes how just thirty birds out of thousands who began the pilgrimage arrive at their sacred destination completely transformed—unrecognizable even to themselves—"without feathers and without wings." Farid ud-Din Attar, *The Conference of the Birds*, translated by C. S. Nott (Shambhala Press, Berkeley, 1971).

143 I came across this amusing term in the following article: "Unidentified Academic Object" by Asad Syrkett, *Architectural Record,* January 2012, Vol. 200, Issue 1, p. 36.

144 During your years of study here you experienced many moments of inspiration, you were guided by distinguished teachers and dedicated tutors, and made friends for life. But you also worked through lonely nights and doubtful days when you were ready to quit, to walk away. Some of you wrestled with drugs or drink, and others with depression, addictions and disease of the body and the mind. Some were isolated, far from home, family and friends, while others always seemed to be popular and partying hard.

145 *Deuteronomy* 6:5; and *cf. Mark* 12:30; *Matthew* 22:36-38.

146  Often attributed to Guillaume Apollinaire (1880–1918), it may actually have been penned by the English poet Christopher Logue (1926–2011).

147  In a number of ancient teachings, including Babylonian, Egyptian, Greek, Hindu and Buddhist, we find the concept that all matter is composed of earth, water, fire, air, and ether. For a general overview of these concepts in various cultures and a discussion on why those theories have been supplanted by Atomic Theory, see *wikipedia.org/wiki/Classical_element*.

148  Shamanic, mystical and magic traditions throughout the world speak of inter-species and inter-phenomena communications. According to Jewish scripture (*1Kings* 4:29-34), King Solomon was the wisest person in the world:
> God gave Solomon wisdom and very great insight, and a breadth of understanding as measureless as the sand on the seashore. Solomon's wisdom was greater than the wisdom of all the people of the East, and greater than all the wisdom of Egypt. He was wiser than anyone else, including Ethan the Ezrahite—wiser than Heman, Kalkol and Darda, the sons of Mahol. And his fame spread to all the surrounding nations. He spoke three thousand proverbs and his songs numbered a thousand and five. He spoke about plant life, from the cedar of Lebanon to the hyssop that grows from walls. He also spoke about animals and birds, reptiles and fish. People came from all nations to listen to Solomon's wisdom, sent by all the kings of the world who had heard of his wisdom.

Legend extended his intelligence to include knowledge of all revealed and esoteric disciplines as well as the ability to communicate with, and control, both natural and supernatural phenomena. Solomon's wisdom, however, did not prevent him from making some character and policy errors during his otherwise illustrious reign.

Kabbalistic tradition taught that the ability to understand the language of Nature was known by at least one person in every generation. See one of the many stories about the Baal Shem Tov (1698–1760), founder of the Hassidic Movement, who was conversant with "The Language of Birds and Animals," *https://breslev.com/265572/*.

## About Yosef Wosk

The Governor General's office described YW as "a Renaissance man of the 21st century" when he was appointed an Officer of the Order of Canada. A member of the Order of British Columbia and a rare recipient of Freedom of the City from the City of Vancouver, he developed the *Philosophers' Café* as one of the largest conversation café programs in the world, attracting more than 110,000 participants since 1998.

In addition to being a Fellow of the Royal Canadian Geographical Society, an ordained rabbi (Yeshiva University) and having received two honorary doctorates, Yosef Wosk holds Ph.Ds in Religion & Literature (Boston University) as well as in Psychology, and masters degrees in Education (Yeshiva) and Theology (Harvard).

A visiting scholar at the Oxford Centre for Life-Writing, he has founded hundreds of libraries on all seven continents, supported museums worldwide, endowed Vancouver's Poet Laureate program and has been involved in the planting of a million trees globally. Cited as a polymath and a rebel brain by *Vancouver Magazine*, Wosk was identified by the *Vancouver Sun* as one of the top ten thinkers in British Columbia.

Having served as a Shadbolt Fellow, Simons Fellow, Adjunct Professor in the Department of Humanities and Director of Interdisciplinary Programs in Continuing Studies at Simon Fraser University, Wosk also gave rise to the *Canadian Academy of Independent Scholars* and he remains active as an art collector, philanthropist and a public speaker. He partnered with Old Massett carver James Hart for many years in the creation of an unparalleled monumental work that combines Haida and Judaic symbols.

Wosk has authored the well-received non-fiction collection *Naked in a Pyramid* (Anvil Press, 2023); he provided the Afterword to *Out of Hiding: The Holocaust Literature of British Columbia* (Ronsdale Press, 2022), winner of the George Ryga Award for Social Awareness; and his correspondence is the main component for *GIDAL: The Unusual Friendship of Yosef Wosk and Tim Gidal* (Douglas & McIntyre, 2022), winner of the Non-Fiction Prize for the Western Canada Jewish Book Awards.

For more information, visit yosefwosk.org

www.ingramcontent.com/pod-product-compliance
Lightning Source LLC
Chambersburg PA
CBHW041308240426
43661CB00038B/1466/J